Praise for *T*

"A great teacher has pro... *Satisfaction* will enrich and challenge in very important ways. This book holds consequential lessons for new believers and lifelong seekers alike. Six of my own novels are based upon the teachings of David McKinley. It is wonderful to see that this fine man and excellent teacher has finally produced a book of his own."

—Davis Bunn
Best-selling Author

"David McKinley has a keen understanding of the human soul. He is also a terrific teacher and storyteller. Combine these elements and the end result is a very significant book. Read *The Search for Satisfaction* and you'll see what I mean."

—Pat Williams
Sr. Vice President, Orlando Magic
Author, *How to be Like Coach Wooden*

"Satisfaction—one word that most aptly describes both our deepest need and our most difficult, often confusing quest. David McKinley leads us past those popularized areas where true satisfaction is never found and into a place where its fullest form is available for each of us. A smooth easy read and an excellent road map for a truly satisfied life."

—Mamie McCullough,
Author and Speaker

"Exploding myths and exploring wisdom, McKinley's *Search for Satisfaction* is must-reading for everyone who wants to build value into their life and impact the lives of those around them. Every leader should read this book!"

—John C. Maxwell
Author, Speaker, & Founder of ISS and EQUIP

"David McKinley's stimulating book contains solid, contemporary answers to mankind's greatest need. I recommend it enthusiastically."

—Dr. George Sweeting
Chancellor Emeritus, Moody Institute of Chicago

"The Search for Satisfaction is an oasis of inspiration for the parched soul. Using Solomon's insights from Ecclesiastes, David masterfully guides the reader to discover the only Source for true contentment in life. I highly recommend this volume to those who are searching for satisfaction in life, as well as those who have discovered it."

—Dr. Robert Jeffress
Pastor and Author, *Spirit Wars*

"With pastoral insight and Holy Spirit direction, David McKinley clearly identifies what is necessary to bring satisfaction to life in a clear-cut, understandable, exciting and encouraging way. His conversational style, as he opens the door of understanding, gives you the distinct feeling he is speaking directly to you—to your heart and to your needs. Beautifully and convincingly written, McKinley reveals the love of God through the wisdom of Solomon, including clear and practical guidelines on what to seek, what to avoid, and how to make wise choices to find the satisfaction we all crave."

—Zig Ziglar
Motivational Teacher and Author, *Better Than Good*

"The Search for Satisfaction" is challenging and inspiring to read causing the reader to reflect about their personal life quest and where to find authentic long-term satisfaction. Here you will find hope and help in practical solutions on how to 'do' life."

—Vonette Z. Bright
Co-Founder, Campus Crusade for Christ, International

"In *The Search for Satisfaction*, David McKinley shows the way to happiness and satisfaction in life. It's the question even history's most successful man, Solomon, wrestled with. The answer? The last place he thought to look!"

—Josh McDowell
Author and Speaker

the search for satisfaction

satisfaction

> looking for
something new
under the sun

David H. McKinley

W PUBLISHING GROUP
A Division of Thomas Nelson Publishers
Since 1798
www.wpublishinggroup.com

THE SEARCH FOR SATISFACTION
© 2006 David H. McKinley

Published by W Publishing Group, a division of Thomas Nelson, Inc., P.O. Box 141000, Nashville, TN 37214.

All Scripture quotations, unless otherwise indicated, are taken from the New King James Version®. Copyright © 1982 by Thomas Nelson, Inc. Used by permission. All rights reserved.

Other Scripture quotations are taken from the following sources: The Amplified Bible (AMP), Old Testament. Copyright © 1965, 1987 by the Zondervan Corporation. Used by permission. All rights reserved. The Holman Christian Standard Bible® (HCSB). Copyright © 1999, 2000, 2002, 2003 by Holman Bible Publishers. Used by permission. The Message (MSG) by Eugene H. Peterson. Copyright © 1993, 1994, 1995, 1996, 2000, 2001, 2002. Used by permission of NavPress Publishing Group. All rights reserved. The New American Standard Bible® (NASB®). Copyright © 1960, 1962, 1963, 1968, 1971, 1972, 1973, 1975, 1977, 1995 by The Lockman Foundation. Used by permission. The Holy Bible, New International Version® (NIV®). Copyright © 1973, 1978, 1984 by International Bible Society. Used by permission of Zondervan. All rights reserved. The Holy Bible, New Living Translation® (NLT®). Copyright © 1996. Used by permission of Tyndale House Publishers, Inc., Wheaton, Illinois 60189. All rights reserved. The New Life Version (NLV). Copyright © 1969 by Christian Literature International. The Living Bible (TLB). Copyright © 1971 by Tyndale House Publishers, Wheaton, Ill. Used by permission.

Cover Design: Brand Navigation
Interior Design: Lori Lynch, Book & Graphic Design, Nashville, TN

Library of Congress Cataloging-in-Publication Data available

ISBN 0-8499-1200-8

Printed in the United States of America
06 07 08 09 10 RRD 9 8 7 6 5 4 3 2 1

To my mom,
Jeanne McKinley—

her eyes never read these words and
her hands never turned these pages, but
her heart helped shaped every thought,
her prayers for me have been realized through this work,
her smile encouraged my faith, and
her example assured me of the
satisfaction found in knowing and following Jesus Christ.

We search the world for truth.
We cull the good, the true, the beautiful,
From graven stone and written scroll,
And all old flower-fields of the soul;
And, weary seekers of the best,
We come back laden from our quest,
To find that all the sages said,
Is in the Book our mothers read.

—JOHN GREENLEAF WHITTIER, MIRIAM

contents

acknowledgments

This book is a work of heart and hands joined together. I share it with gratitude to my family, mentors, churches, and friends who have contributed to my own spiritual growth and life development.

I am grateful for Connie, my faithful life partner. Her devoted love and positive support provided the confidence and encouragement I needed to see my yearning for this book fulfilled. What we believed when we started we have proven day by day: "Two are better than one" (Eccles. 4:9). You are the love of my life.

I am blessed by the presence of Joseph and Mary Elizabeth in my home. They are gifts from the Lord and have added daily to the satisfaction Connie and I share together. No dad could have greater pride or joy in his children.

I must thank Tracey Drake, my ministry assistant, whose creative energy and commitment to excellence in all things have lifted my teaching ministry to a higher level. No task has been too great and no detail too small for her attention and care. Thank you, Tracey.

I am amazed how a brief word of encouragement in a hallway encounter with Debbie Wickwire, my editor, opened this door of opportunity. From a business card to a book—what a journey! Thank you, Debbie.

I add a final word of honor and gratitude to the memory of my pastor, Dr. Adrian Rogers, who stepped into heaven a few short weeks before the completion of this work. His strong voice, godly example, and satisfied life provide fuel for my walk with Christ and service each day. I took a picture with him in Israel many years ago and overlaid it with these words: "As for you, David, continue in the things you have learned and been assured of, knowing from whom you have learned them (2 Tim. 3:14)."

And, as I have signed every letter throughout my ministry, it is my prayer that this work will be "unto the praise of His glory."

Foreword

Every person is on a search for life at its best. We desperately want our lives to matter. Yet so often our days are full but not fulfilling. Emptiness is the common condition of our culture. As a result, many wonder if it is possible to find real satisfaction.

I am a part of a generation that grew up in the sixties listening to Mick Jagger's Rolling Stones sing, "I can't get no satisfaction . . . I've tried and I've tried, but I just can't get no satisfaction." After all these years, it is still considered the number one rock song of all time, the cry of a generation that tried it all and came up empty.

Centuries ago, God spoke through the life of a man who represents every man. His name was Solomon. He recorded his life story in a kind of spiritual journal known as Ecclesiastes. Though it is an ancient writing, it is as current as your life today because it describes our search for significance and satisfaction and then offers the solution, which is found only in a relationship with the one true God.

David McKinley describes this journey into life with the skillfulness of a surgeon, the heart of a preacher, the wisdom of a scholar, and the creativity of an artist.

You, like everyone else on the planet, want your life to be meaningful. You desire something more than everything under the sun you have experienced. You may have given up the search, thinking it is impossible to find genuine peace and purpose. Let me assure you, you will find in this powerful book answers to your questions and truth for living.

You hold in your hands a life-changing book. It is not an accident that you picked it up. In fact, if you will read and think deeply about what is within these pages, you will discover satisfaction that will last forever.

So get ready! David McKinley is about to take you on the adventure of your life. What you are about to experience is not theoretical but believable, livable, and doable. The principles of God's Word are true. If you will trust Him and follow Him, your life will not only make sense but also make a difference. There is no limit to your life if you will live it God's way. You are about to find what you have been looking for your entire life: satisfaction.

—DR. JACK GRAHAM
Pastor, Prestonwood Baptist Church, Plano, Texas

the search for satisfaction

Out, out brief candle!
Life's but a walking shadow, a poor player
That struts and frets his hour upon the stage,
And then is heard no more. It is a tale
Told by an idiot, full of sound and fury,
Signifying nothing.

—WILLIAM SHAKESPEARE, *MACBETH* (5.5.25-30)

chapter 1

living in search mode

Ecclesiastes 1

Every day, I go through the same routine.

With a few strokes on my keyboard and the click of a mouse, I travel through a global gateway into a world of interaction and information. My "commute" via the Internet is similar to a rush-hour drive, merging with masses and moving through a variety of points of passage called URLs, Web sites, and home pages.

The curious thing about this daily pattern is that it doesn't matter where I am, who I am with, or how I am dressed. All I have to do is summon my search engine, and I am empowered to connect and communicate on the global information highway. So, day after day, it is the same. Boot up. Log on. Select an engine. Start a search.

Oftentimes, routine searches only lead to frustration. I don't find solutions; I simply wander in search mode, wasting time, energy, and effort. I click here. Go there. Read this. Look at that. I link. I think. I log out. I walk away disappointed by my lack of success. And I wonder why I give time to such trivial pursuits, wishing I had started with a clearer plan.

One day, I realized that what I experience in my daily Internet search routine has become a way of life for many. People face each new day, hitting the Enter key to search or plug in words and phrases with the hope of finding satisfactory solutions for life. They, too, are powered by search engines. Not necessarily Google, Yahoo, or the likes of Dogpile, but their engines are revving deep within to search for greater satisfaction in life. People want answers, experiences, and contacts that will change the way they live and view life. They live in search mode. People long for a day when they will encounter someone or something that will lead them to a fuller and more meaningful life.

Can you relate?

People long for a day when they will encounter someone or something that will lead them to a fuller and more meaningful life.

Have you ever had an itch on your back you couldn't scratch? You stretch your arm over your shoulder. You can't get there. You twist it up behind you, but there is still no relief. You enlist the aid of another only to find that their assistance adds to your frustration. You can't satisfy the agitation. Maybe even reading about it has you squirming right now.

Or what about the trip to the fridge at the end of the day? Maybe you enjoyed an evening meal, but later that night you find yourself searching for something that will satisfy. You move to the pantry and try a handful of crackers. A cookie? Some chips? You nibble. You munch. But when all is said and done, your search ends without satisfaction.

We all know people who live with "itches" they can't scratch.

They go from experience to experience, from relationship to relationship, from place to place, and from project to project without resolution. We know people who live with a gnawing sense that life is not satisfying, but they don't know what they want or where to look to find a solution. They seek guidance, growth, and gain only to find unsatisfactory results. They live in search mode, yet their search yields only disappointing results day after day after day.

Life soon echoes the mantra of Mick Jagger, that great British philosopher whose proclamation soared to the top of the charts: "I can't get no satisfaction!" Yet forty years later, the Stones and many of their fans are still searching for satisfaction. The name of their latest world tour, A Bigger Bang, says it all. Like many of us, the Stones are still looking for something *more*.

How Can Anyone Find True Satisfaction?

In the fall of 2004, television ratings soared for ABC with the introduction of *Desperate Housewives*, a sizzling series depicting women who live in upscale suburban homes and wear designer clothes but are frustrated by their empty hearts. Their manicured lawns and orderly lives are only a facade to hide their confusion. These housewives are beautiful people with hungry souls desperate to find satisfaction.

And so it goes.

Earlier this year, I had the opportunity to speak with three former NFL players. Each enjoyed a Super Bowl experience during his career. One was inducted to the Dallas Cowboy "Ring of Honor" at Texas Stadium. Yet in each conversation, I heard the same refrain: "Success did not bring lasting satisfaction. The key thing to life is purpose, and I searched for that in football. I got to a place where I had money, success, and all that went with it. But I was frustrated. Life was complicated, and I was not a good husband, father, brother, or person. My motivation to achieve did not result in lasting satisfaction."

We read of the young and restless, the new wave of "tweens" who have greater purchasing power than the previous generation of adolescents. Yet these kids are filled with angst to know and understand what really matters in life.

We hear of Hollywood stars whose luminary excess only brings them distress. They are bombarded daily by a feeding frenzy of fans and photographers who are obsessed with every detail of their lives. In the end, most celebrities struggle to understand why all of their assets provide only illusions of happiness. Listen to how French actress and sex symbol Brigitte Bardot described her life of beauty and wealth: "I have been very happy, very rich, very beautiful, much adulated, very famous . . . and very unhappy." And actor Harrison Ford admitted the ultimate futility of fame: "The actor's popularity is evanescent—applauded today, forgotten tomorrow."

We observe people day after day going through the mundane routines of life, and we wonder, *How can anyone find true satisfaction?*

From the suburbs to the inner cities, from thriving cultural centers to rural landscapes, people are on a desperate search. They long to find a relationship that will complete them, to acquire a possession that will add value to them, to enjoy an experience that will change them, or to gain a greater knowledge that will enable them to move from search mode to satisfaction. In words that ring all too clearly in the minds and hearts of my generation, "I try . . . and I try . . . and I try . . . and I try . . . I can't get no sat-is-fac-tion!"

Are You Living in Search Mode?

Can I get personal? Do you find yourself frustrated by your life's direction or lack thereof? Are you searching for something but not sure what it is or how to find it? Is "search mode" the defining characteristic of your life?

Let me introduce you to a man who has reflected and written extensively on the subject of search-mode living. His name is

Solomon. He was the worldly, wise, and wealthy king of Israel who described search-mode living as the ultimate reality experience "under the sun."

Throughout history, Solomon has worn the moniker "Wisest Man Who Ever Lived." Yet this wise and wealthy king relates candidly his own struggles to find satisfaction in life. Without the aid of a word processor or an electronic database, Solomon penned a journal of life reflections and conclusions.

We observe people day after day going through the mundane routines of life, and we wonder, How can anyone find true satisfaction?

It is interesting to note that Solomon's life journal begins with a bold and depressing assertion. Let's take a moment to consider it:

> Smoke, nothing but smoke. . . . There's nothing to anything—it's all smoke. What's there to show for a lifetime of work, a lifetime of working your fingers to the bone? One generation goes its way, the next one arrives, but nothing changes—it's business as usual for old planet earth. The sun comes up and the sun goes down, then it does it again, and again—the same old round. The wind blows south, the wind blows north. Around and around and around it blows. . . . Everything's boring, utterly boring—no one can find any meaning in it. Boring to the eye, boring to the ear. What was will be again, what happened will happen again. There's nothing new on this earth. Year after year it's the same old thing. (Eccles. 1:2–6, 8–9 MSG)

Another translation of his final assessment says, "Everything is so weary and tiresome! No matter how much we see, we are never satisfied. No matter how much we hear, we are not content. History merely repeats itself. It has all been done before. Nothing under the sun is truly new" (Eccles. 1:8–9 NLT).

After reading this passage, you might feel like saying, "Pass the Prozac!" If you are like me, you wonder if you want to read any more "inspirational thoughts" from Solomon's journal. His "life seminar" doesn't exactly sound like the kind of gathering you want to devote a weekend to for personal growth.

Solomon's words are frustrating, cynical, and irritating. From deep within, the reader cries out, "Surely there's more!"

At the same time, we have to admit that Solomon's words echo the unsatisfied feelings of people through the ages. T. S. Eliot once said, "We humans cannot bear very much reality!" I think he is right. Though we don't like the cynical reflections of Solomon's search, many of us can identify with the monotonous experience of living in search mode. And the truth is, we don't like it! No matter how hard we try to find answers or apply an advanced search, life seems like a repetitive merry-go-round—and we know all the horses by name. We are empty. We are bored. We grow tired of the search.

Though we don't like the cynical reflections of Solomon's search, many of us can identify with the monotonous experience of living in search mode.

What should we do? There are days when our longing for satisfaction doesn't really matter. We just live to enjoy the moment. We laugh a little and go on with life. But there are days when this gnawing frustration—this unresolved search—calls us to seek answers. How do we respond? Should we stop and admit it? Should we deny, suppress, or seek to escape it?

The fact is, most of us go on living desperate lives only to echo Solomon's conclusion about life "under the sun." We point, click, connect, link; look, hope, buy, and sell—only to find ourselves star-

ing at a blinking cursor on the screen of our lives with a message
that reads, "Your search returned no results."

Solomon is not the only person to express such reflection and
dissatisfaction with life. In *Walden*, Henry David Thoreau wrote,
"The mass of men lead lives of quiet desperation." I would para-
phrase this to say, "Most people lead lives of active dissatisfaction."

*Many have reflected on life only to observe that sometimes there
is less out there than meets the eye.*

We get busy. Life intensifies. Yet beneath all the speed, noise,
and activity—beyond the roles, responsibilities, and relationships—
we still struggle with dissatisfaction. Let's see what a few others
have said about this subject.

British poet Matthew Arnold observed, "Most men eddy about
here and there—eat and drink, chatter and love and hate, gather and
squander, are raised aloft, are hurl'd in the dust, striving blindly,
achieving nothing; and then they die." And H. L. Menken said, "The
basic fact about human experience is not that it is a tragedy, but that
it is a bore."

Dare I continue? These are not exactly encouraging words; you
won't see them imprinted over picturesque landscapes and framed
in offices.

After reading these observations, Solomon doesn't sound so bad
after all. All these echoes of gloom only serve to remind us that
many have reflected on life only to observe that sometimes there is
less out there than meets the eye.

Most lives are not marked by vices; they are simply lived with no
purpose. And for the human soul, nothing is more horrific than the
thought of living and dying in vain. Did I mention that the most common refrain in Solomon's journal is "Vanity of vanities, all is vanity"?

These negative observations could lead us to despair. But Solomon did not say life is only full of sadness and suffering. He did say life "under the sun" lacks sense and satisfaction. Thirty-seven times in his life-management seminar, Solomon uses words such as *vanity*, *meaningless*, and *not satisfied* to communicate his idea of emptiness.

Finding Proofs for a Life That Matters

The Greek philosopher Socrates said, "The unexamined life is not worth living." So I want to invite you to take an exam. I know you may despise any thought of testing, but tests help you discover proofs for life. It certainly applies to the water you drink, the food you eat, the car you drive, and the home in which you live. It is even likely that the clothing on your back bears a tag included by Inspector #9.

Solomon did not say life is only full of sadness and suffering. He did say life "under the sun" lacks sense and satisfaction.

Tests assure quality and value in life. Doesn't your life (the most valuable thing you possess) deserve an examination? Wouldn't you like to find some "proofs" for a life that matters?

Maybe you are thinking, *I can't add much to old King Solomon. I've already read enough of his evaluation to get depressed.* I know. I had those same thoughts too. Then I discovered something about Solomon's journal: I spent enough time in his life-management seminar to discover that he wasn't so despairing after all.

Solomon started his journal with a bleak conclusion so he could take us on his journey to find a new beginning of hope and satisfaction.

chapter 1

living in search mode

How Can Anyone Find True Satisfaction?

Every day, people fill the "search bar" of their lives with random yet routine searches in hopes of finding something new under the sun.

When you do a life search, you, too, may discover:

- Observation will make you skeptical.
- Experience can make you cynical.
- Knowledge can make you fearful.
- Life leaves you doubtful.

Are You Living in Search Mode?

In the book of Ecclesiastes, the wise and wealthy King Solomon relates candidly his own struggles to find satisfaction in life.

"Everything is so weary and tiresome! No matter how much we see, we are never satisfied. No matter how much we hear, we are not content. History merely repeats itself. It has all been done before. Nothing under the sun is truly new" (Eccles. 1:8–9 NLT).

The book of Ecclesiastes tells us that life *under the sun* is fuel for a desperate journey:

"Vanity of vanities, *all* is vanity" (Eccles. 1:2, emphasis added).

"Everything is meaningless . . . utterly meaningless!" (Eccles. 1:2 NLT).

"It is of no use! All is for nothing" (Eccles. 1:2 NLV).

"Absolute futility. Everything is futile" (Eccles. 1:2 HCSB).

Many of us can identify with the monotonous experience of living in search mode. And the truth is, we don't like it!

Finding Proofs for a Life That Matters

Wouldn't you like to find some "proofs" for a life that matters?

In this journal of his own search for satisfaction, Solomon started at the end to help us find a new beginning.

Truth sits upon the lips of dying men.

—MATTHEW ARNOLD, "SOHRAB AND RUSTUM," 1853

chapter 2

no matches found

Ecclesiastes 1

Time magazine featured an article in January 2005 entitled "The New Science of Happiness: What Makes the Human Heart Sing?"[1] The article discussed how psychologists often focus on symptoms of mental illness rather than essential qualities of mental health and well-being.

In the article, Martin Seligman, the former president of the American Psychological Association, said, "I realized that . . . it wasn't enough for us to nullify disabling conditions and get to zero. We needed to ask, 'What are the enabling conditions that make human beings flourish? How do we get from zero to plus five?'" (© 2005 Time Inc., Reprinted by permission) Dr. Seligman called for psychologists to focus on characteristics that express happiness, satisfaction, and fulfillment in life.

Seligman's interest had been piqued by the research of Dr. Edward Diener, aka "Dr. Happiness," who developed a "satisfaction with life scale" to assess common qualities identified in those who lived on the "plus-five" side of mental health.

How satisfied are you with your own life? Take a look at Dr. Diener's scale, and see how you rate:

Satisfaction with Life Scale

Below are five statements that you may agree or disagree with. Using the 1–7 scale below, indicate your agreement with each item by placing the appropriate number on the line preceding that item. Please be open and honest in your responding.

7—Strongly agree   3—Slightly disagree
6—Agree   2—Disagree
5—Slightly agree   1—Strongly disagree
4—Neither agree nor disagree

_____ In most ways, my life is close to my ideal.
_____ The conditions of my life are excellent.
_____ I am satisfied with my life.
_____ So far I have gotten the important things I want in life.
_____ If I could live my life over, I would change almost nothing.

35–31—Extremely satisfied   15–19—Slightly dissatisfied
26–30—Satisfied   10–14—Dissatisfied
21–25—Slightly satisfied   5–9—Extremely dissatisfied
20—Neutral

So how did you do? Anyone get a score of "extremely satisfied"? If so, you are one of the few who has discovered the secret that Solomon learned in his own search for satisfaction. But if you're like most people, your score is a bit lower on the satisfaction scale, and you're still living in search mode.

Think about your own life. What makes you happy? How do you move into the "plus-five" category? The opinions, suggestions, and pursuits vary from person to person and place to place. What would it take for you to find satisfaction? Have you examined and established your own "plus-five" ideal?

Solomon's "Satisfaction with Life Scale"

The curious thing about the research published in the *Time* article is that our wise friend Solomon scooped the story. He developed his own "satisfaction with life scale" and recorded his observations and experiences in his life journal. Solomon was quick to expose some of the common myths of meaning being espoused in his day and ours.

Solomon published his findings on ancient papyrus more than two thousand years ago. Yet his observations are as cutting-edge as those published in *Time*, which utilizes the latest versions of today's electronic data systems.

Solomon was quick to expose some of the common myths of meaning being espoused in his day and ours.

Sitting at my keyboard, I watch the cursor blink as I pause to collect my thoughts. It awaits my next motion, command, or action. This also occurs when I engage Google, Yahoo, or other popular search engines to receive my request and take me to my desired destination. There have been days, however, when I entered a word, a phrase, or a question only to receive the simple reply, "No matches found."

Five Myths of Satisfaction

Solomon also compiled a list of five searches that had no match in his "satisfaction with life scale." Let's put our search engine in motion and see what Solomon discovered.

Search #1: Progress

Many people today feel that their lives will be significant if they can expand their horizons and enlarge their opportunities through advancement in education and technology. They long to surpass former generations in exploration, innovation, and creative design. To them, the sky is the limit.

No generation in history has witnessed the explosion of knowledge and technology we experience today. Processing components have become smaller while the horizon of possibilities has expanded. We are all beneficiaries of progressive innovation. Each day, I become aware of new technology that creates a new tool for business, commerce, or communication. Phones and photographs, customized songs for individual callers (such as music from a Star Wars soundtrack signaling the entrance of Darth Vader when Dad calls), and the ability to connect globally through satellite phones all provide a broad base of knowledge and awareness that exceeds the grandest dreams of former generations. Yet knowledge, information, awareness, and our sense of "connectedness" have not issued in a glorious age of peace. To the contrary, all of this progress has only added to our sense of vulnerability.

Yet knowledge, information, awareness, and our sense of "connectedness" have not issued in a glorious age of peace.

As I write these words, I can hear in the background news reports of massive damage and destruction as a result of Hurricane Katrina along the U.S. Gulf Coast. This natural disaster caused devastation in greater proportion than our country has ever experienced because progress allowed expansion, development, and settlement in regions once thought uninhabitable. Today, pictures are projected in real time as the human drama unfolds, and millions wonder how the advances that so often seem to secure our lives can so quickly threaten our well-being.

Solomon insightfully observed, "Much learning earns you much trouble. The more you know, the more you hurt" (Eccles. 1:18 MSG). Knowledge increases worry and sorrow. Our explosion of knowledge has resulted in an escalation of concern. The more we know, the more we fear.

We have advanced in knowledge, yet we increase our frustration because we cannot assimilate that knowledge into satisfactory results.

Solomon had a royal library of knowledge that would shrink in comparison to the data available at your fingertips. However, that did not limit his understanding of or insight into the limitations of progress to resolve present human problems.

We have advanced in the knowledge of medicine, climate, agriculture, health, fitness, and even relationships. Yet we increase our frustration because we cannot assimilate that knowledge into satisfactory results. Did I mention that the researcher in *Time* magazine observed, "Sorry, Mom and Dad, neither education nor, for that matter, a high IQ paves the road to happiness"?[2]

Solomon perceived the limitations of progress in the realm of satisfaction.

His search on "progress"? No matches found.

Search #2: Excess

Party on! Surely the pursuit of happiness goes through a town called Pleasure. Solomon thought so. In fact, he decided to remove his inhibitions and live life without a rule book. "I said to myself, 'Come now, let's give pleasure a try. Let's look for the 'good things' in life" (Eccles. 2:1 NLT). He didn't want to hurt anyone; he simply wanted to take it all in—and he did!

Solomon's pursuit of excess was probably at least as lavish as, if not more lavish than, the spending habits of Swaziland's King Mswati III, who recently purchased ten BMW 5 Series cars for his wives as Valentine's Day gifts. The expense of the gifts, valued at just under $1 million, was added to his own indulgence of a $500,000 luxury car he purchased for himself. In addition to his ten wives, the king has three fiancées. King Mswati's spending habits have resulted in a series of protests in a nation in which over 70 percent of the total population live on an average income of $1 or less each day. And beyond these national protests, can you imagine the personal challenge that King Mswati faces every day as he tries to keep ten wives and three fiancées happy?

Like this modern king, Solomon tried to find satisfaction in wine, women, and song. But when the music stopped and the food grew stale, when the wineskins were empty and the women were gone, when the friends had departed and Solomon was alone, he wrote, "I found that this, too, was meaningless. 'It is silly to be laughing [partying] all the time,' I said. 'What good does it do to seek only pleasure?'" (Eccles. 2:1–2 NLT).

Excesses may gratify temporarily, but gratification and satisfaction are not the same.

Solomon's search on "excess"? No matches found.

Search #3: Success

Solomon's search led him to do a benefit analysis on success in life. He was convinced after the "wasted" experiences of excess that doing something meaningful for himself and beneficial for others would bring the satisfaction he deeply craved.

Like many in our day, Solomon decided to press, climb, sacrifice, and focus on success. And history records the success of his leadership and expansion. Here's how Solomon recorded his own view of the journey: "Anything I wanted, I took. I did not restrain myself from any joy. I even found great pleasure in hard work, an additional reward for all my labors. But as I looked at everything I had worked so hard to accomplish, it was all so meaningless. It was like chasing the wind. There was nothing really worthwhile anywhere" (Eccles. 2:10–11 NLT).

From many successful people, I heard the same refrain: "If my life is so full, why do I feel so empty?"

I have had the opportunity to live in communities surrounded by people who have gained pinnacle successes and made outstanding contributions. I have lived on the outskirts of the "fantasy island" of Palm Beach, Florida; and I have enjoyed the big, bold, and bodacious spirit of Texas while living in North Dallas. I have served as a pastor within minutes of SpacePort USA (Kennedy Space Center) and an hour's drive from the gateway to the Magic Kingdom, and then as a pastor of a wonderful church in Boca Raton, arguably the jewel of Florida's Gold Coast. In each community I met people whose phenomenal talent and accomplishments provided success beyond their highest hopes and dreams. Yet in each place and from many successful people, I heard the same refrain: "If my life is so full, why do I feel so empty?"

How tragic to get where you want but to hate it once you get there!

Solomon echoed this emptiness. His search on "success"? No matches found.

Search #4: Possessions

Maybe we could finally be satisfied if we could just get a little more. You know the motto "Get all you can, can all you get, sit on the lid, and poison the rest." This may be overstated, but it is easy to get caught in the trap of thinking that material gain will bring lasting fulfillment. But as the *Time* article points out, "Once your basic needs are met, additional income does little to raise your sense of satisfaction in life."[3]

Solomon had houses and lands, horses and treasures. He was a man of phenomenal wealth in the ancient world. He built the temple, the centerpiece of Israel's worship and the showpiece of the city of Jerusalem until it was destroyed in 587 BC. The ruins of his wealth and possessions can still be viewed in Israel today. But listen to these haunting words: "Those who love money will never have enough. How absurd to think that wealth brings true happiness! The more you have, the more people come to help you spend it. So what is the advantage of wealth—except perhaps to watch it run through your fingers!" (Eccles. 5:10–11 NLT).

Incredible! You can be saturated with *stuff* and still be dissatisfied with life. The lesson is clear: money doesn't buy happiness, health, wholeness, or satisfaction. At least the poor have the hope of having more, but the rich have it and know what they don't have.

The lesson is clear: money doesn't buy happiness, health, wholeness, or satisfaction.

I have been fascinated to read about men and women who won lotteries only to add to their life burdens. In her article "Unlucky in Riches," Ellen Goodstein notes, "Having piles of cash only compounds problems for some people." In this article, Goodstein relates "sad tales of foolishness, hit men, greedy relatives, and dreams dashed."[4]

One victim of his own possessions was William "Bud" Post, who won $16.2 million in the Pennsylvania lottery. He later lamented, "I

wish it never happened. It was totally a nightmare." He was sued,
assaulted, misled, deceived, and ultimately ended up over $1 million
in debt. At the time of the story, he had declared bankruptcy and
was living on $450 a month with food stamps. While you may think
this a freak occurrence, this same article related eight such stories of
soaring cash flow and tragic loss.

Search results on "possessions"? You guessed it! No matches found.

Search #5: Impression

"I want to leave a legacy." What words could express a nobler
ambition? We know that first impressions linger. But is there a lasting impression that will satisfy our need for significance?

> *Is there a lasting impression that will satisfy our need for significance?*

Recently I learned that Bill Gates, the richest man in the world—
the man whose name identifies his socioeconomic status, "Billionaire"—along with his wife, Melinda, has established the largest
nonprofit foundation in the world. Their foundation is intended to
turn their limitless profits from progress in technology into philanthropy. This is a noble and worthy goal. It clearly identifies a desire
to move beyond success to significance. The Bill and Melinda Gates
Foundation is aimed at "promoting greater equity in global health,
education, public libraries, and support for at-risk families," as stated
in the headline of their foundation Web page.[5] It would seem Bill
and Melinda want the Gates name to move beyond product association to people and a purpose that matters. But does philanthropy
lead to lasting satisfaction in life?

Solomon observed, "A good name is better than precious ointment, and the day of death than the day of one's birth; better to go

to the house of mourning than to go to the house of feasting, for that is the end of all men; and the living will take it to heart" (Eccles. 7:1–2).

When *progress*, *excess*, *success*, and *possessions* did not bring the results Solomon hoped to find, he thought about *legacy*. Solomon wrote in Proverbs 22:1, "A good name is to be chosen rather than great riches, loving favor rather than silver and gold." Was Solomon maturing? Had he eliminated his personal indulgences in hopes of a lasting impression? It would appear a noble and philanthropic thing to do.

How can we have so much to live with and yet struggle to find something to live for?

While Solomon understood and affirmed the positive virtue and extended value of philanthropy, he recognized his best efforts to aspire to significance would take him to the common end of all men, death. Men may leave a legacy, but they cannot escape the inevitability of their own death. Death shadows even our best ambitions to live for something that will ultimately matter.

Solomon's search on "impression"? No matches found.

The Fatal Flaw in Solomon's Search

How can we have so much to live with and yet struggle to find something to live for? This was the dilemma that haunted Solomon until he realized that his search had one fatal flaw: he had limited his search to life under the sun. His limited search engine had exhausted its capacity. It was not until Solomon changed and enlarged his search that he began to get results in his quest for satisfaction.

Maybe we, too, should expand the boundaries of our search.

no matches found

Solomon's "Satisfaction with Life Scale"

More than two thousand years ago, Solomon developed his own "satisfaction with life scale" and recorded his observations and experiences in his life journal.

Five Myths of Satisfaction

In the book of Ecclesiastes, Solomon uses the "search engine" of personal experience to expose five common myths of satisfaction.

Search #1: Progress

"Much learning earns you much trouble. The more you know, the more you hurt" (Eccles. 1:18 MSG).

Increased knowledge and new technology have not issued in a glorious age of peace. To the contrary, all of this progress has only added to our sense of vulnerability.

Search #2: Excess

"'Let's give pleasure a try. Let's look for the "good things" in life.' But I found that this, too, was meaningless. 'It is silly to be laughing all the time,' I said. 'What good does it do to seek only pleasure?'" (Eccles. 2:1-2 NLT).

Excesses may gratify temporarily, but gratification and satisfaction are not the same.

Search #3: Success

"I even found great pleasure in hard work, an additional reward for all my labors. But as I looked at everything I had worked so hard to accomplish, it was all so meaningless. It was like chasing the wind" (Eccles. 2:10-11 NLT).

From many successful people, I have heard the same refrain: "If my life is so full, why do I feel so empty?" How tragic to get where you want but to hate it once you get there!

Search #4: Possessions

"Those who love money will never have enough. How absurd to think that wealth brings true happiness! The more you have, the more people come to help you spend it. So what is the advantage of wealth—except perhaps to watch it run through your fingers!" (Eccles. 5:10-11 NLT).

You can be saturated with *stuff* and still be dissatisfied with life.

Search #5: Impression

"A good name is better than precious ointment, and the day of death than the day of one's birth" (Eccles. 7:1).

Leaving a lasting impression does not satisfy a need for significance in life.

The Fatal Flaw in Solomon's Search

Solomon searched extensively for satisfaction—only to find that the result of his search was "No matches found." But his search was limited to life under the sun. He looked around, but he didn't look up.

*Life is what happens to you while
you're busy making other plans.*

—John Lennon, "Beautiful Boy (Darling Boy)"

life happens!

Ecclesiastes 3

J ust imagine the possibilities behind the two-letter word *if.*
Imagine *if* tomorrow morning and every day thereafter for the
rest of your life you were promised a daily deposit of 86,400 pennies
in your operating account. Pause to do the math, and you quickly
discover that this adds up to $864 a day. It would compound to
nearly $6,000 per week and over $315,000 a year for the rest of your
life. Not bad pocket change. Would you be a taker?

With the promise of this daily deposit comes one absolute and
unalterable stipulation: you have to spend every penny every day.
There is no accumulation, no accrual, and no compounded interest. You simply spend it or lose it. It would be quite a challenge,
wouldn't it?

If you step out of the world of imagination and into the realm
of reality, you do receive this exact deposit of "change" each day. It
is called *time.* There are 86,400 seconds composing the 24 hours of

each of the 7 days of every week of the 365 days you live each year of your life.

With this realization comes a strategic understanding of the importance of time. Each day, you choose how to use your time or you lose it. As it has been said, "Life is like a coin. You can spend it any way you want, but you can only spend it once." As you search for satisfaction, you have to deal with the daily trade-offs you make with your time. In those trade-offs, you can discover solutions to make life matter.

In his life journal, Solomon voiced an assumption I believe you would endorse: better time management results in better life fulfillment.

Benjamin Franklin said, "Value time, because it is the stuff that life is made of." Because time is such a valuable commodity, any discussion of how to find lasting satisfaction in life will surely take us past the "Big Ben" of time management. So it does not surprise us that in Solomon's search to find satisfaction, he not only pursued experiences for fulfillment, but he reflected on the importance of time.

In his life journal, Solomon voiced an assumption I believe you would endorse: *better time management results in better life fulfillment.* Have you ever considered this? Do you think this is true?

Because of our focus on speed and schedules, we have a tendency to think we are the only society to struggle with intense time-management issues. The fact of the matter is that all we have really added to life in our day are speed and noise. We have not added to or diminished the twenty-four hours in a day. The time you have today is the same as that experienced by Solomon in the ancient world. Although he did some pretty incredible things, Solomon shared in the same 86,400-seconds proposition that you and I are given every day.

To Everything, Turn, Turn, Turn . . .

One of the best-known expressions on the subject of time came from Solomon. Many do not know it is a portion of Scripture. In fact, we sing it as we scan through "golden oldies" from the '60s. It goes like this:

> To everything, turn, turn, turn,
> There is a season, turn, turn, turn
> And a time for every purpose under heaven. . . .[1]

Do you recognize it? Do you remember who sang it? The Byrds. Where did they get their thoughts and lyrics? Solomon!

Solomon recorded these thoughts in his life journal and then provided us with some amazing insights for our life search on the subject of time. If I had to summarize, I would simply say, "Life happens!" Day after day, season after season, life moves in perpetual progression. You cannot save time, store time, or change time. You can only use it wisely or waste it foolishly.

In the summer of 2004, I received a phone call while attending a board meeting at Palm Beach Atlantic University. The meeting was an add-on to a wonderful beach vacation my family spent in a condo shared with us by dear friends in Central Florida. We spent eight long, lazy days reading, swimming, and enjoying life "under the sun." Connie; our daughter, Lizzi; and her friend Christina flew back to Dallas at the end of our vacation time together while I drove south to West Palm Beach to attend the trustee meeting.

My days of summer fun came to an abrupt halt as I answered my cell phone and listened to Connie's strained voice on the other end: "Something has happened to your mom. Your dad found her just a few minutes ago. She's confused . . . not normal response . . . taking her to the hospital . . ." My mind raced as I tried to grasp the situation and determine my next move.

Within a short time I was on a plane headed to Memphis, Tennessee, hurrying home to see Mom; help Dad; join my brother, Rick; and offer support.

What had taken less than three minutes to communicate by phone changed everything for the next eighteen days. A series of emotional ups and downs finally brought me to the first stanza of Solomon's reflection: "A time to be born, and a time to die."

On July 18, 2004, I said good-bye to my mom. It's strange how the moment of death ushers in a surge of silence, a stillness no one wants to disturb with movement or time. It's a sense that once words are uttered, the moment has passed and time continues without the one you love.

In the days that followed, our extended family and friends joined my family in a tearful reunion. A service of honor and remembrance was led by our beloved pastor, Dr. Adrian Rogers, whose faithful encouragement through the Scriptures offered hope. We made our way to the cemetery, where my dear friend and pastor, Jack Graham, expressed final words of affection and comfort. He and his wife, Deb, had been on a special trip that ended with a long flight from Europe to be with us. I will never forget their effort to join us at that graveside. Finally, we turned to walk away.

Hours later, we stepped out of that place of seclusion and back into the sudden and unimpeded pace of life. While our world changed in a moment, the world at large moved on in time.

Time doesn't stop—not when we grieve or when we fail, when we hurt or when we stumble. Life happens. It keeps going and going and going. Nor does it stop when we win, no matter how grand or glorious. Do you remember who won the Super Bowl last year? Can you name the best actor or actress at last year's Academy Awards? Do you know who won the Nobel Peace Prize?

Life happens. From piercing moments of injury to the highest moments of achievement, life keeps moving forward day after day after day. No matter how perilous the hour you may be facing or how exhilarating the moment you may be experiencing, your own life journal will record the entry . . . and then you turn the page.

The Sequence of Life

Solomon captured something of the sequence of life. He presented it in stanzas and couplets in Ecclesiastes 3:1–11, using a form of poetry called *Hebrew parallelism*. While most of our poetic material is distinguishable by rhyme and meter, the poetic style of ancient Hebrew was a parallel completion of thoughts and ideas, each contrasting with or complementing one another. You find this extensively in the writings of King David, Solomon's father, when you read portions of Scripture like Psalm 119.

To help you understand this form of poetry, let me show you a few examples of the *completion*, *complement*, or *contrast* of thought in Hebrew parallelism:

- *Completion:* "Blessed are those who keep His testimonies, [then comes the completive and expansive thought] who seek Him with the whole heart!" (Ps. 119:2). Again, "Your word I have hidden in my heart, [completive thought] that I might not sin against You" (Ps. 119:11).
- *Complement:* "Your word is a lamp to my feet and a light to my path" (Ps. 119:105). *Lamp* and *light* are both complement and completion. The second thought completes the first.
- *Contrast:* "The proud have forged a lie against me, [then the contrast] but I will keep Your precepts with my whole heart" (Ps. 119:69).

Now let's review the reflections of Solomon as he expresses them in the beauty of Hebrew parallelism—contrast and completion. As you read these familiar lines, pause to consider Solomon's insights of spiritual wisdom:

To everything there is a season,
A time for every purpose under heaven:

A time to be born,
    And a time to die;
A time to plant,
    And a time to pluck what is planted;
A time to kill,
    And a time to heal;
A time to break down,
    And a time to build up;
A time to weep,
    And a time to laugh;
A time to mourn,
    And a time to dance;
A time to cast away stones,
    And a time to gather stones;
A time to embrace,
    And a time to refrain from embracing;
A time to gain,
    And a time to lose;
A time to keep,
    And a time to throw away;
A time to tear,
    And a time to sew;
A time to keep silence,
    And a time to speak;
A time to love,
    And a time to hate;
A time of war,
    And a time of peace.

What profit has the worker from that in which he

labors? I have seen the God-given task with which the sons of men are to be occupied. He has made everything beautiful in its time. Also He has put eternity in their hearts, except that no one can find out the work that God does from beginning to end. (Eccles. 3:1–11)

Solomon expresses a breakthrough in thought and understanding as he begins to see life in light of God's order and design rather than his own.

Thirty times Solomon uses the word *time* in these brief verses. It is almost as if you can hear the *tick, tick, tick* of the clock. Solomon observes our awareness of and desire for understanding of what life in time is all about. He ultimately relates an important insight concerning the nature and meaning of time. Rather than seeing time as a tragedy—unfolding with each change of season and turning of the page—he observes the order and significance of time.

Solomon expresses a breakthrough in thought and understanding as he begins to see life in light of God's order and design rather than his own. His search for satisfaction through acquisitions and experiences has turned up empty, so now he expands his search from external surface issues to find a deeper, inner significance. Solomon's own search for significance (just like yours and mine) is inseparably linked to time and our awareness of it.

We divide our lives and measure them by increments of time. Unlike the animal kingdom moving with the rhythms of changing seasons, we make every attempt to measure, reflect, and invest our time so as to make life count. It is this obsession with time that leads to a pursuit of significance. We need to know that there is reason and purpose for the time and space we occupy on planet Earth. We are not content to let the sun rise and set without discovering meaning or significance in life. Solomon's search moved beyond success and experience to significance because of his awareness of time. He observed the happenings of life and realized his own clock was ticking. With this came a heightened awareness and compelling desire to find meaning in the life he lived.

As Solomon communicates his thoughts, he makes one insight clear: while life may at times appear chaotic, life is not chaos. Life happens, but life is not just happenstance. Life is a series of ups and downs. Life is a progression of changing seasons. It is a sequence of events, experiences, and evidences of something more than what we see under the sun. It is this reality in all of the seasons of life echoed in Ecclesiastes 3:11: "He [God] has put eternity in their hearts, except that no one can find out the work that God does from beginning to end."

Life happens, but life is not just happenstance.

What an idea! Our search here, now, today—our seasons, good, bad, or otherwise—all take us to a place where we must look beyond the sun to find solutions. This is going to take a bigger search engine than we ever imagined!

life happens!

Every day, you receive an exact deposit of *time*—86,400 seconds. As you search for satisfaction, you have to deal with the daily trade-offs you make with your time.

"Life is like a coin. You can spend it any way you want, but you can only spend it once."

In his journal, Solomon observed that *better time management results in better life fulfillment.*

To Everything, Turn, Turn, Turn . . .

"To everything there is a season, a time for every purpose under heaven: a time to be born, and a time to die; a time to plant, and a time to pluck what is planted; a time to kill, and a time to heal; a time to break down, and a time to build up; a time to weep, and a time to laugh; a time to mourn, and a time to dance; a time to cast away stones, and a time to gather stones; a time to embrace, and a time to refrain from embracing; a time to gain, and a time to lose; a time to keep, and a time to throw away; a time to tear, and a time to sew; a time to keep silence, and a time to speak; a time to love, and a time to hate;

a time of war, and a time of peace" (Eccles. 3:1-8).

Day after day, season after season, life moves in perpetual progression. You cannot save time, store time, or change time. You can only use it wisely or waste it foolishly.

The Sequence of Life

Solomon expresses a breakthrough in thought and understanding as he begins to see life in light of God's order and design rather than his own.

As Solomon communicates his thoughts, he observes that while life may at times appear chaotic, life is not chaos. Life is a series of ups and downs, a progression of changing seasons.

The sequence of life reveals that there must be something more than what we see under the sun.

Time is really the only capital that any human being has, and the only thing he can't afford to lose.

—THOMAS EDISON, INVENTOR

my clock is ticking

Ecclesiastes 3

For more than a quarter century, most U.S. government wall clocks have come from one place: the Chicago Lighthouse. And to the surprise of many, it is an organization whose primary focus is employing the blind. During the 1940s and '50s, Lighthouse events included the heroic and inspirational Helen Keller, along with some of America's leading philanthropists. The Lighthouse has had quite a history and is now approaching its centennial birthday.

However, a recent article on the front page of the *Wall Street Journal* bore the title "Time Running Out for Clockmakers in Chicago."[1] The article indicates that Chinese markets are providing stiff competition for the Chicago Lighthouse. It appears these markets employ laborers for a fraction of the cost of American workers and can produce a larger volume of standard brown wall clocks at a lower cost. The article discusses the contributions of the

Chicago Lighthouse operations through the years and the efforts being made to "beat the clock" in the current wave of competition.

As I read the article, I thought about the common interest we all share in managing our time and adjusting to the competing forces we face every day. From Solomon's "lighthouse" for life navigation found in Ecclesiastes 3, we discover some important insights for living.

Time Reflects Order

First, Solomon demonstrates how ultimate reality is found in the way time reflects order. Remember our earlier discussion? While life can be downright chaotic, life in the larger sphere does not reflect chaos. Life is not a random experience; it has pattern, purpose, and design.

Life is not a random experience; it has pattern, purpose, and design.

Life happens, but it is not accidental. Are there things in life we can't explain? Absolutely. Does life cause us to question our meaning, worth, and importance? Sure. Do we struggle to reconcile the things we cannot understand with the things we do? No doubt. But in the big picture, the order of life's cycles and seasons reminds us that life is not simply a random operation.

Life reflects design, sequence, and order. Thus, any search to find satisfaction in life will always take us to the shoreline of reflection on our own significance. *Why am I here? Am I merely part of the ongoing process of natural selection and cultural progression?* Solomon's response assures us that this absolutely is not so.

Though our journey through Solomon's writings began with a conclusion that bordered on fatalism (which is "the belief that all

events are determined by fate and, therefore, inevitable"[2]), Solomon
states that the sequential order of time does not allow us to embrace
the idea that life is merely a series of accidental occurrences strung
together before we die. No, time reflects order.

Let's take a moment to consider the first of the couplets presented in Solomon's prose: "A time to be born, and a time to die"
(Eccles. 3:2). This statement reflects the bookends of life under the
sun. We begin with a baby book and close with a book of remembrance. Whenever you exit planet Earth, your grave will bear a
marker of time—a tombstone or memorial plaque. What is found
on most? The dates of your birth and death. Life is what happens in
the "dash" between the two.

We all have a desire to know and understand the significance of
life. We want to know that what happens in the "dash" on our tombstone is something of value, meaning, and importance. This is a cru-
cial mark of distinction between the animal kingdom and humankind.

Animals look down to the ground for subsistence and existence.
They follow their instincts and drives. People, on the other hand,
look up. Through the ages of recorded history, men and women have
looked with wonder at the stars and the heavens to understand their
own significance and to discover the meaning of their existence.

Years ago, I heard a sermon entitled "Why I?" This is truly the
question of the ages for all humankind. Though we may individu-
ally appear as a speck of sand on the shores of time, we cannot help
but yearn to know and understand the meaning of life. The reality
of birth and death leads not to fatalism but rather to realism that
what happens in between matters.

Now let's return to consider the remaining sequences
Solomon presents to help us embrace the reality of order in a
world of chaos. Everything has its time. As we read the brief yet
comprehensive couplets of thought of Ecclesiastes 3:1–8, we mar-
vel at the wisdom Solomon exhibits in expressing order in the perpetual motion of life.

Time Reveals Outcome

Next, Solomon's reflections encourage us to consider this thought: time reveals outcome.

Solomon shifts his attention in Ecclesiastes 3:10–11: "I have thought about this in connection with the various kinds of work God has given people to do. God has made everything beautiful for its own time. He has planted eternity in the human heart, but even so, people cannot see the whole scope of God's work from beginning to end" (NLT).

Because of the inherent value of the time we receive, we must manage our time so that we can live our lives on purpose.

If all we see in life is order, we will be exasperated. The movement and progression of life is more than something to experience. There is a bigger picture. It is in this moment that we begin to see new ideas dawning in Solomon's mind and heart. He says life under the sun will never make sense. If we only view life from under the sun, our view will be inadequate and limited. There is something inside of each of us that pushes us to understand more.

We all search for ways to reconcile the seasons of life with our need for a purpose that makes daily experience matter. We believe there must be more to life than we are experiencing, but we wrestle to know how to turn such belief into experience and practice.

Time Requires Oversight

Finally, Solomon challenges us to remember that time requires oversight, or management. Because of the inherent value of the time we receive, we must manage our time so that we can live our lives on purpose.

Are you living "on purpose," or have you given your life over to the random acts of occurrence—wishing, hoping, and yearning for a sudden discovery in your daily search for satisfaction? Solomon challenges us to make life decisions and to choose life directions that will enable us to find solutions in our search. He concludes, "Whatever God does, that's the way it's going to be, always. No addition, no subtraction. God's done it and that's it. That's so we'll quit asking questions and simply worship in holy fear. Whatever was, is. Whatever will be, is. That's how it always is with God" (Eccles. 3:14–15 MSG).

Starting today, you can revise your search. You can, and dare I say *must*, reckon your time clock with God's calendar. Why? Because your life is not yours alone. You were made for God's purpose and plan. Note the key component in Eccles. 3:11: "He has put eternity in their hearts." This is the "missing link" in the discovery of life's meaning and satisfaction. We will never find direction in our life search until we come to the conclusion that we were created by a God who put us in a time sequence and order.

Starting today, you can revise your search. You can, and dare I say must, reckon your time clock with God's calendar.

Each of our lives is included in the statement, "He has made everything beautiful in its time" (Eccles. 3:11). Any search we engage in absent of this key perspective and vital component will leave us navigating through life along a dark and treacherous shoreline without illumination and hope.

While Solomon's search continues beyond the words found in

this portion of his journal, he does provide us with a pivotal point of reference for future updates in our own search for satisfaction.

Five Ways to Maximize Your Days[3]

Before I close this chapter, I want to offer several tips I have discovered to help me manage my own clock. I first heard these insights on making time count from my pastor and mentor, Dr. Adrian Rogers, who for thirty-two years led Bellevue Church in Memphis, Tennessee.

Dr. Rogers related the following insights from a familiar verse in the Psalms often quoted in public gatherings of worship: "This is the day the LORD has made; we will rejoice and be glad in it" (Ps. 118:24). I share these insights with you in order to help you improve your clock management and enhance your own life search.

1. *View each day as a gift from God.* Seeing life as a gift rather than a sentence will change everything about the way you live it. Tragically, the drudgery and monotony of life can cause us to drift and become despondent. Clarifying this focus at the beginning of each day will help you to be grateful for the "little things" in life.

2. *Live in the present tense.* Someone has said, "The two days that can take the joy out of today are yesterday and tomorrow." It is easy for us to become frustrated by yesterday's failures and anxious about tomorrow's uncertainties. Living in the present tense enables us to live life to the fullest today.

3. *Set priorities for each day.* Just as time reflects order, it is in ordering your life that you find significance and satisfaction. Failing to plan is planning to fail. Being inattentive to the priorities of your life is a sure way to gain a disposition of dissatisfaction.

4. *Refuse to procrastinate.* "Procrastination is the thief of time," said Edward Young. Instead of waiting, postponing, and delaying, we need to adopt a "Do it now!" mentality. This is more than a compulsive motto. It is a prescriptive strategy for life satisfaction.

5. *Choose to enjoy today*. Just as you receive this day as a gift from God, live this day to the fullest. And what is the secret? Make a choice about today. Choose to enjoy it. Don't live in misery by default. Live with intentionality. While you cannot control the circumstances of this day, you can choose the disposition you bring to it.

"Time Is Chasing All of Us"

J. M. Barrie is a world-renowned author, playwright, and story-teller. He was one of seven children born to a common Scottish weaver. At age seven, Barrie dressed up in the clothing of his deceased brother, David, who was killed in an accident, and tried to cheer the broken heart of his mother. His efforts at role playing would shape the mind and genius of the man who would later write one of the most beloved of all stories, *Peter Pan*. In 1904, *Peter Pan* was first performed at the Duke of York's Theater in London, and the rest is history.[4]

In 2004, the life story of J. M. Barrie's struggle and ultimate rise to success was retold in the heartwarming movie *Finding Neverland*. The movie reflects the real-life events and experiences that shaped the creative facets of Barrie's style. In this movie, there is a scene in which Mr. Barrie is introduced to Mr. and Mrs. Snow, an older couple who were admirers of his work and regular attendees at his opening-night performances.

We cannot search for meaning in life without being aware of the value of time.

In the movie, when the Snows first meet Barrie, they demon-strate a courteous yet cautious expression of appreciation for his work, even though it was evident to most that his play was a bomb.

Yet sometime later, on the opening night of *Peter Pan*, Mr. Barrie encounters Mrs. Snow following the enthusiastic and thunderous reception of all those in attendance. When Barrie inquires about her husband, Mrs. Snow tells Barrie of his passing. She goes on to report what joy Mr. Snow would have found in Peter Pan because he was a man who never really grew up. Then she adds, "It's like the ticking clock in the alligator in your play. . . . Time is chasing all of us."

Suddenly from Barrie's portrayal of fantasy comes a resounding message of reality. We cannot search for meaning in life without being aware of the value of time.

Time goes you say? Ah no! Alas, Time stays, we go.
—HENRY AUSTIN DOBSON

chapter 4

my clock is ticking

We all have to manage our time and adjust to the competing forces we face every day. From Solomon's "lighthouse" for life navigation found in Ecclesiastes 3, we discover some important insights for living.

Time Reflects Order

The order of life's cycles and seasons reminds us that life is not simply a random operation.

Ecclesiastes 3:1–8 shows us that there are many "seasons of life":

- To be born and to die
- To plant and to harvest
- To kill and to heal
- To tear down and to rebuild
- To cry and to laugh
- To grieve and to dance
- To scatter stones and to gather stones
- To embrace and to turn away
- To search and to lose
- To keep and to throw away
- To tear and to mend
- To be quiet and to speak up
- To love and to hate
- For war and for peace

Time Reveals Outcome

We all search for ways to reconcile the seasons of life with our need for a purpose that makes daily experience matter.

"God has made everything beautiful for its own time. He has planted eternity in the human heart, but even so, people cannot see the whole scope of God's work from beginning to end" (Eccles. 3:11 NLT).

Time Requires Oversight

Because of the inherent value of the time we receive, we must manage our time so that we can live our lives on purpose.

"Whatever God does is final. Nothing can be added to it or taken from it. God's purpose in this is that people should fear him. Whatever exists today and whatever will exist in the future has already existed in the past. For God calls each event back in its turn" (Eccles. 3:14–15 NLT).

Five Ways to Maximize Your Days

- View each day as a treasured gift from God.
- Live in the present tense.
- Set priorities for each day.
- Refuse to procrastinate.
- Choose to enjoy today.

"Time Is Chasing All of Us"

You cannot search for meaning in life without being aware of the value of time.

If anyone thinks himself to be something,
when he is nothing, he deceives himself.

—GALATIANS 6:3

"do-it-yourself" attitudes

Ecclesiastes 4

A new religion has emerged during the past two decades in America. Each week, thousands of patrons make their weekly pilgrimage to the growing number of temples built across the sprawling landscape of our cities and suburbs. The followers of this new religion are not content to merely come and see; they want to go and do what they have discovered during their weekly gatherings in the temple.

These emerging shrines are the expressions of America's new-found faith in "do-it-yourself" endeavors. And the patrons are "week-end warriors"—men and women alike who make it their aim to prove themselves worthy and faithful to the mission of the do-it-yourself religion. The rising success of home-improvement stores like Home Depot and Lowe's evidence our innate desire to prove our personal competence through do-it-yourself expression.

In addition to these highly visible stores, an entire cable channel,

DIY, is dedicated to do-it-yourselfers. And Web sites abound to propagate the faith of this rapidly growing religion. Sites like Handyman USA, the Install Doctor, Ms. Builder, Roofhelp.com, SoYouWanna.com, Tipztime, and . . . Toiletology 101, which boasts of a class participation averaging more than twenty-five hundred students each day. On this unique site, you are invited to "take a seat, plunge in, flush out the facts, and plumb the depths of toilet repairs."

Yes, the do-it-yourself religion is spreading far and wide across our country. I must admit, I have been influenced by the do-it-yourself creed. I have considered converting on several occasions, but to date, I am not fully persuaded. The reasons for my unbelief are many. But among them are the experiences I have had with ceiling fan installation, basic electrical repairs, simple plumbing, and worst of all, painting and wallpapering.

I will never forget when we moved into a new home several years back. It was our first time to build a house, and it was a positive and enjoyable experience. The home was delivered fully equipped with the latest and greatest appliances, cabinetry, countertops, and fixtures, and we picked basic neutral colors for the walls and interior. Our home was beautifully landscaped on the outside, and our yard was laid in a day, with no patching or waiting required since we lived in Florida at the time.

After living in our new home for several months, Connie and I decided to accent the home with some personal touches of color and décor. We spent several days searching for paint colors and wallpapers that would enhance the beauty of our home. I will never forget the day we found a limited number of rolls of a high-quality, brilliant red wallpaper that seemed perfect for a small guest bathroom in our living area. I thought, *How hard could this be?* Taking a small step of faith, I launched into what I perceived to be a low-risk, high-impact, minimal time commitment to transform a small white room into an awesome thing to behold.

I started my simple do-it-yourself project after dinner around seven in the evening. The bathroom could not have been more than six feet by six feet. Armed with a wallpaper tray and glue, I took the plunge into the bathroom. The first three walls were finished within an hour or so. The only thing that took time was some basic cutting and trimming around the entry door.

But the back wall, the one where the toilet sat, proved to be my nemesis. For the next four hours, I faced the frustration of uncooperative cuts around a mirror, the obstruction of plumbing fixtures, and finally, the realization that my great deal on a limited number of rolls of high-end paper would cost me more time and frustration than I ever could have imagined.

You guessed it: I ran out of paper and found myself digging through scraps, matching patterns, and trying to create my own wallpaper jigsaw to fit and finish the wall that was most predominant when you entered the room. I recall that it took some twenty to thirty cuts of small shapes and slivers of paper to finish my project. For years, when I walked into that room, I doubted my ability to ever succeed at another do-it-yourself endeavor.

Much of our trouble in life begins with a do-it-yourself attitude.

What have I learned? *Be careful what you convince yourself you can do alone.* You may be self-deceived. Much of our trouble in life begins with a do-it-yourself attitude. We are driven to demonstrate our independence and competence through our best do-it-yourself efforts.

I remember well how my children would often squirm and shout when Connie or I tried to do things for them they would rather do themselves. As toddlers, they would protest, "No, me! I do it," when they felt ready to take charge of their world. Yet we don't always leave this mentality behind in maturity. Even though experience and knowledge add much to our personal capabilities, we all have a need to prove we can survive, withstand, and demonstrate that we can handle anything. We fear just asking for assistance is a weakness.

Reckon with Your Relationships

Our friend Solomon made this same observation centuries ago. While journaling personal insights in his search for satisfaction, he brushed the ever-sensitive nerve of our need for personal relationships. He tried to reconcile the tension between our search for personal satisfaction and a world that challenges us to live beyond ourselves. Any true search for satisfaction includes investigation in the realm of interpersonal relationships. It's an inescapable issue. We are surrounded by people and involved in relationships. The question is, how do you view, value, and verify your friendships in life?

Any true search for satisfaction includes investigation in the realm of interpersonal relationships.

Solomon's cynicism surfaced as he wrote: "Then I observed that most people are motivated to success by their envy of their neighbors. But this, too, is meaningless, like chasing the wind" (Eccles. 4:4 NLT). In other words, too many relationships are simply races. They are used as a means to measure our own value by comparing our achievements with the achievements of others. Instead of being complementary, these friendships are competitive. Solomon says, "If all I am doing is beating my neighbor, then this is a fool's game."

Solomon expands the thought in Ecclesiastes 4:7–8: "Again I saw something meaningless under the sun: There was a man all alone; he had neither son nor brother. There was no end to his toil, yet his eyes were not content with his wealth. 'For whom am I toiling,' he asked, 'and why am I depriving myself of enjoyment?' This too is meaningless—a miserable business!" (NIV).

As I read these words, the name Howard Hughes surfaced in my mind as a modern image of this ancient inscription. Hughes, the first American billionaire, is an American icon. However, his inquisitive mind, innovative endeavors, and independent spirit could not satisfy his deepest needs. He was linked to legendary Hollywood "babes" Katharine Hepburn, Bette Davis, Jean Harlow, and Ava Gardner. Yet his independent and self-absorbed tendencies led to a trail of broken hearts and lost loves. Howard Hughes was the personification of high profile and high achievement, but he was also a man who searched for satisfaction.

By the late 1950s, Hughes had become a total recluse. His compulsive tendency to be a "do-it-yourselfer" contributed to his obsessive fear of germ contamination through human contact. His drug-afflicted life led him to isolation and destruction. In his final years, Hughes shuttled between hotels in Beverly Hills, Boston, and Las Vegas, trying to avoid public attention. And in the end, he became a victim of his own eccentricities.[1]

"This also is vanity and a grave misfortune," says Solomon (Eccles. 4:8). Self-absorption is a sure way never to find satisfaction.

While Solomon's search for solutions has yielded little thus far, one thing is sure: you have to reckon with your relationships. You cannot go it alone. You need people, and, I might add, people need you.

One thing is sure: you have to reckon with your relationships. You cannot go it alone.

Our world is enamored with celebrity and stardom, and we tend to elevate individuals as ideals of success, beauty, and achievement. But the fact is that no one is fully self-made or fully self-fulfilled.

Apart from growing and lasting relationships with others, our lives are empty, lonely, and, to use Solomon's favorite word, *vain*.

It is as though Solomon is saying, "Let me warn you about self-absorption. I want you to know that if you achieve individual success and leave other people out, you will always lack satisfaction and fulfillment in life. Winning isn't all it's built up to be. Achieving is not just a solo thrill. Recognition without relationship is a one-way ticket to Lonely Street and the Heartbreak Hotel. One clue to finding true satisfaction in life is recognizing that you will never make this discovery alone."

Confront the Myth of the Lone Ranger

John Maxwell writes, "As much as we admire solo achievement, the truth is that no lone individual has done anything of value. The belief that one person can do something great is a myth. . . . Even the Lone Ranger wasn't really a loner. Everywhere he went he rode with Tonto!"[2]

Could it be you are our own worst enemy in your search for satisfaction? Are you neglecting one vital discovery surfaced by Solomon: the need for a little help from your friends?

We have to confront the myth of Lone Ranger thinking in our search to find satisfaction. Why? Because our personal search will never satisfy our deep need for the connectivity that leads to contentment.

Therefore, the virus in our search is often nothing more and nothing less than our own pride. When a spirit of pride dominates us, we will soon discover all of life becomes a push and a panic to outdo and overcome the competition of others. Pride is the fuel of an empty life, as we will explore more fully in the next chapter.

"do-it-yourself" attitudes

For some reason, we are driven to demonstrate our strength through independence. We seem to be born with a resistance to assistance.

Reckon with Your Relationships

Solomon tried to reconcile the tension between our individual search for significance and a world that challenges us to live beyond ourselves.

"I observed that most people are motivated to success by their envy of their neighbors. But this, too, is meaningless, like chasing the wind" (Eccles. 4:4 NLT).

"I saw something meaningless under the sun: There was a man all alone; he had neither son nor brother. There was no end to his toil, yet his eyes were not content with his wealth. 'For whom am I toiling,' he asked, 'and why am I depriving myself of enjoyment?' This too is meaningless—a miserable business!" (Eccles. 4:7–8 NIV).

You have to reckon with your relationships. You cannot go it alone. You need people, and people need you.

Confront the Myth of the Lone Ranger

"As much as we admire solo achievement, the truth is that no lone individual has done anything of value. The belief that one person can do something great is a myth. . . . Even the Lone Ranger wasn't really a loner. Everywhere he went he rode with Tonto!" —John Maxwell

We have to confront the myth of Lone Ranger thinking in our search to find satisfaction.

Our personal search will never satisfy our deep need for the connectivity that leads to contentment.

Life is a long lesson in humility.

–JAMES M. BARRIE, *The Little Minister*, 1891

chapter 6

pride and precipice

Ecclesiastes 4

I once delivered newspapers. It was not the Americana experience of a youngster throwing newspapers while maneuvering a rickety bicycle across grooved sidewalks. And it was not my first job. In fact, it was an enterprise I engaged in while in graduate school. I was married, had a college degree, and ran a paper route. The demands on my time for class schedules and extended study required a job with flexible hours. It's hard to get more flexible than four o'clock in the morning. You only have one major competitor—sleep!

For more than two years, I threw nearly 386 copies—give or take a subscription—of the *Commercial Appeal*, a daily newspaper in Memphis, Tennessee. I was on the job seven days a week. It was a challenging job both physically and financially. Physically, I learned the true meaning of a power nap. Sometimes it was the "napsters" that held my life together. Financially, I learned you could collect enough money to pay the paper bill and still not collect your profit for your work. In layman's terms, "You can work for nothing!"

Yet during these days, I learned a hard but important lesson. It was not easy at first, but today I share it with great pride and gratitude.

One morning while I was waiting for the delivery truck to make a "drop" with my papers, I noticed the headlights of a familiar car heading my way. I looked up to see my dad's face behind the steering wheel. My first thought was that something was wrong, but he quickly assured me he had come to lend me a hand. He told me I might need a backup on occasion. If he learned the route, he could help me whenever needed.

My dad was an insurance agent. He had a full-time job and a busy schedule. I quickly (and sharply) reminded him that I was grown, married, and capable of doing it by myself. But my protest did not deter him.

Morning after morning, I remember seeing those headlights appear in that dark, cold parking lot during those years. Each time, I remember feeling my pride trapped in the headlights of his love and care. The only thing (apart from lack of sleep) that added to the stress of those days was my own attitude of aggravation fueled by my pride in the face of my father's love.

I can still hear him say, "I enjoy this. It makes my day go better." I'd think, *Yeah, right! Sleep deprivation is anything but the way to add value to your day.* But my dad determined to help me, despite the wounds his efforts brought to my own pride.

Pride is the fatal flaw in our relationships with others.

Today, I wouldn't trade anything for a father who was willing to wound my pride to show his love. Today I can think of only two words that I failed to repeat with frequency in those days: "Thanks, Dad!"

PRIDE: A Disease of the Soul

Pride. It's amazing how pervasive and progressive this disease is in the human soul. Pride is the fatal flaw in our relationships with others. It brings competition, tension, obstruction, and conflict. "By pride comes nothing but strife," says Solomon in his wisdom book (Prov. 13:10).

Pride is deceitful in nature. It is disgusting on parade. It is disrespectful of the grace of God and the gifts of others. Pride is a dangerous, poisonous agent in the human soul. Pride destroys.

None of us is as sure-footed as we like to think. Pride undermines our steps and will always take us to the precipice of danger and destruction.

The Bible warns us concerning the deceitful and destructive power of pride. "Pride goes before destruction, and a haughty spirit before a fall" (Prov. 16:18). And again, "Therefore let him who thinks he stands take heed lest he fall" (1 Cor. 10:12). None of us is as sure-footed as we like to think. Pride undermines our steps and will always take us to the precipice of danger and destruction.

You might be thinking, *I thought pride was a good thing. Shouldn't we take pride in our work, in the well-being of our children, in the achievements of others we love, and in the blessings of our nation?* Of course. The pride I am talking about is not the good kind. It's like cholesterol: there is good and bad. HDL cholesterol is good. It aids and helps the heart to perform its vital functions. Sufficient levels of HDL will actually prevent a heart attack. But there is the

bad cholesterol, LDL. This is an agent of obstruction that can clog
and cut off from arteries vital blood flow essential for survival.

So it is with pride. The presence and abundance of the "bad kind"
of pride can and will clog your heart and kill your relationships.

Five letters align to form a word on the Scrabble board of life and
define the fatal flaw in our relationships: PRIDE. Pride creates
obstruction, competition, tension, and conflict in your relationships.
If you focus on the middle letter of the word *pride*, you quickly discover that many people struggle to get along with others because of
"I" trouble. Their view of life is tainted by obsession with themselves.

Karen, my sister-in-law, once overheard and passed this little
confession my way. "When I was in my twenties, I spent all my time
worrying about what people thought of me. I dressed, I talked, and
I acted in ways that would make people think the best of me. But
when I got to my forties, I took on a new perspective. I decided that
I didn't care what anybody thought about me. Being worried about
other people's opinions only added to the stress and frustration of
an overcrowded life. But then I hit my sixties. And suddenly I made
the greatest discovery of all. Nobody was ever thinking about me in
the first place!"

Revealing, isn't it? How often do you let your preoccupation
with yourself keep you from focusing the best of your energies and
attention on others and on things that matter most?

For many years, I have shaped thoughts and ideas in the form of
acrostics to help me remember and communicate with others. I sup-
pose I first mastered this tool to help me get through tests in school.
Over time, it has become a bit of a game to help me maintain focus
and progression in my speaking. I enjoy teaching, building, and shap-
ing a series of thoughts out of one key word in my text or message.

Because of the latent power found in pride, I want to use PRIDE
as an acrostic and hope this bit of wordsmithing will challenge you,
as it has me, to do some personal investigation to see if you need to
get rid of pride.

Preoccupation with Self

When you are puffed up with pride, all of your attention and concentration are on yourself. Think about the example Solomon cited in the last chapter. He achieved much, but he was detached from other people. He had many associations but no deep or intimate relationships. What could be worse than to aspire and achieve, only to end up alone, with a life that is empty and meaningless?

Resistance to Assistance

You may often think, *I can't and won't let others know I have needs or need them.* It is this resistance to assistance that keeps you at arm's length from the very people and interactions that can make all the difference in your life.

If you have ever walked into a crowded room needing to find a seat, you know the awkward and even humorous gesturing that can occur. Another attendee enters simultaneously, and each of you encourages the other to take the last remaining seat. However, ten minutes later you are both still standing and the chair is still empty! Some people would rather have a need go unmet than to admit their need.

In Ecclesiastes 4:8, the laborer was compulsive about work, effort, and energy. But at the end of the day, and even more at the end of his life, he was still standing alone.

Pride prevents you from experiencing the love of God and sharing His love with others.

Isolation in Fear

Pride causes you to disconnect and detach. Instead of engaging with others, you distance yourself from people out of fear. You think that if people get close enough, they may realize you are not all you are hyped up to be. The presence of such fear isolates you from the risk of relationships and the potential for growth through intimacy with others.

Fear will isolate you from your mate in marriage. Fear can injure relationships in your business. Fear can destroy communication and vital connectedness with your children. When fear is present, it consumes you and keeps you from the prevailing power of love. For this reason, the apostle John pointed out, "Perfect love casts out fear" (1 John 4:18). This is the love God has for you. Pride prevents you from experiencing the love of God and sharing His love with others.

Do you live day after day without satisfaction or fulfillment because you are unwilling to face "fear factors" in your relationships due to the clogging of pride and all of the symptoms that go with it? Like the laborer whom Solomon describes in his journal, do you keep climbing but never find true contentment? "There is no end to all his labors, nor is his eye satisfied with riches. But he never asks, 'For whom do I toil and deprive myself of good?'" (Eccles. 4:8).

Solomon had been so caught in the grip of his own greed that he ended up with the grit of an empty life.

Division Through Greed

Pride has a cousin named *greed*. Greed is gain at the expense of others. It is a life strategy like that of the man Solomon referenced that involves loving things and using people rather than loving people and using things. However, the end of all greed is loneliness and emptiness. Grace and gratitude draw people to you, but greed repels people. Solomon had been so caught in the grip of his own greed that he ended up with the grit of an empty life.

Erosion in Relationships

Pride destroys relationships. In a powerful and pointed way, Solomon writes, "By pride comes nothing but strife" (Prov. 13:10). Arguments, fights, and disputes often come down to a battle of wills. Ego squares off with ego, and the result is erosion in your relationships. Pride is not a builder but a destroyer. It is like a termite in your soul. While its presence is not easy to perceive, its damage can be devastating.

Develop a "We" Focus

So what should you do? It all begins with focus. Just as you can shift your focus from place to place in a room or view the vast expanse of a blue sky or the detailed elegance of a spring flower, so you must be intentional to change a self-focused life.

The smaller your sphere of influence is, the lesser your legacy in life. You don't have to have much to have great influence. Mother Teresa is a good example of this. But you do have to give much to have great influence. If you put too much emphasis on your own importance, your life will wither. It is only when you extend the gift of your life rather than exaggerate the importance of your life that you maximize your impact and experience the joys of a life that matters.

I have heard Zig Ziglar say on many occasions, "You can get everything in life you want if you will just help enough other people get what they want." He also says, "The secret to your success is making others successful."[1] I think Zig's got it! He is a living example of a man whose love for adding value to others has given him value and favor with people all over the world.

Even as I write these words, Mr. Ziglar is in India extending his legacy of love. And did I mention he turns seventy-eight on his next birthday?

A breakthrough moment in life always comes the moment you quit thinking and living in the limited realm of "I" and start walking in the world of "we." When life is "we focused," it breaks free from the perilous and painful bonds of pride.

So what have we learned? What is Solomon saying? You will never be fulfilled or satisfied if you attempt to go it alone. Friendships matter, but pride destroys and separates friends. In a clear and succinct way, Solomon said it like this: "Pride goes before destruction, and a haughty spirit before a fall. Better to be of a humble spirit with the lowly, than to divide the spoil with the proud" (Prov. 16:18–19).

When it comes to the matter of satisfaction in life, friendships matter!

What was Solomon's eulogy of the rich man's life? "This also is vanity and a grave misfortune" (Eccles. 4:8). The rich man had a great fall. He fell off the wall of his own success.

When it comes to the matter of satisfaction in life, friendships matter!

pride and precipice

Pride is the fatal flaw in our relationships with others. It brings competition, tension, obstruction, and conflict.

The Bible warns us concerning the deceitful and destructive power of pride:

"Pride goes before destruction, and a haughty spirit before a fall" (Prov. 16:18).

"Therefore let him who thinks he stands take heed lest he fall" (1 Cor. 10:12).

"By pride comes nothing but strife" (Prov. 13:10 NIV).

PRIDE: A Disease of the Soul
Preoccupation with Self
Resistance to Assistance
Isolation in Fear
Division Through Greed
Erosion in Relationships

Develop a "We" Focus
"You can get everything in life you want if you will just help enough other people get what they want."
—Zig Ziglar

When life is "we focused," it breaks free from the perilous and painful bonds of pride.

When it comes to the matter of satisfaction in life, friendships matter!

Don't walk in front of me—
I may not follow:
Don't walk behind me—
I may not lead.
Walk beside me—
And just be my friend.

—Unknown (often attributed to Albert Camus)

the friendship factor

Ecclesiastes 4

I t was March 3, 1979, just past eleven o'clock in the morning. Earlier, the skies had been turbulent with storms over the Memphis skyline. Sunlight began to break through as blustery winds swirled and clouds scattered. We stood approximately three miles east of the mighty Mississippi River. I remember the circumstances and conditions well, because on this day I established a partnership and embraced a *friend for life*.

The event to which I refer actually took place in a church with a beautiful young woman named Connie Hall standing at my side. In a moment of holy passion, we made promises to God and each other. She linked her future and identity with me. The love of my life became my wife. This partnership by marriage has made all the difference in my life and, I might add, in my own search for satisfaction.

Like many couples in our day, we wore earth tones. The formal black and white tuxes were displaced by the styles of the 1970s:

velveteen bow ties affixed to brown tuxes, peach dresses, poufy hair, and music that included both a lone singer with a guitar and, of course, a church organ. We were young, idealistic, ambitious, and broke.

Connie had just completed nursing school. I was on the near edge of what would be a decade of higher education. Yet together we were ready to take on the world.

In the days leading up to our wedding, we followed the traditional practice of sending invitations to our guests. The invitation bore these words:

> Two are better than one, because they get more done by working together. If one falls down, the other can help him up. But it's bad for the person who is alone and falls, because no one is there to help. If two lie down together, they will be warm; but a person alone will not be warm. An enemy might defeat one person, but two people together can defend themselves. A rope that is woven of three strands is hard to break.

Where did we find such expression? Solomon. Having described the emptiness of achievement without relationships in Ecclesiastes 4:8, Solomon makes a sudden shift in his focus and perspective in verse 9. He says relationships are a vital part of everyone's search process.

Consider the Value of a Partner

From the sad story of a lonely man's existence to a bright light of discovery, Solomon declares that friendships and partnerships do make a difference in the satisfaction and security of our lives. To put it in the words of author and speaker Gary Smalley, "Life is relationships; the rest is just details."[1]

Good, healthy relationships strengthen who you are and what you do in life. You need to share the pathway of life even if you take "the road less traveled," whether with a spouse or with close friends.

Life achieves greater value and balance in tandem than it does solo.
I believed this in March 1979, and today I know the reality of this discovery more than ever before.

Do you remember the rocketlike success of *Who Wants to Be a
Millionaire*? It was the rage for several seasons in television ratings.
One evening, while watching a contestant answer a series of ascend-
ing questions toward the grand prize of one million dollars, I remember hearing the question, "How many booster rockets are there on a
space shuttle?" The clock was ticking. The guy in the hot seat was
struggling. He obviously did not know. Suddenly I was shouting out
loud at the television, "Two! Two! TWO!" I felt very frustrated that
my answer and his opportunity could not find common ground.

You see, I lived in Merritt Island, Florida, for six and a half years.
Merritt Island is the residential community on the south end of an
inland island on the Atlantic seaboard where the Kennedy Space
Center is located. Space shuttle launches were a routine way of life in
that community, and I watched scores of shuttle liftoffs and landings.

On launch days, I would follow a shuttle liftoff to the distant
edge of the horizon. One unique feature of a live launch is that in
the final moments of viewing, you can often observe the two
booster rockets as they separate from the body of the spacecraft and
begin their descent back to the Atlantic Ocean.

Speaking of view, I have a confession to make. I realize I share
this event at the risk of incriminating myself, but early one morning
just before dawn, I went with a group of men from my church to do
some offshore fishing. It was a launch day in our community, and
the shuttle was scheduled for liftoff just after sunrise. I loved the idea
of getting a new perspective on a launch. We made our way out
through Port Canaveral in the predawn hours and could only see sil-
houettes on the water as we started fishing several miles from the
coast. We were listening to radios and monitoring the dramatic
moments of the countdown.

The Coast Guard and Air Force worked together to secure the

air and water space within a prescribed distance of the launch. This secure zone was highly sensitive, and any violations threatened the sequence of the launch (and, I might add, invited prosecution for criminal trespassing).

As the NASA spokesman narrated the final minute of the launch, my friends took their pastor and friend hostage. They started the engines and soared with wide-open abandonment toward the restricted water area.

Your life will never find maximum impact without partnership.

My heart was racing. I was imagining the headlines in *Florida Today* the next morning: AREA PASTOR LEADS RENEGADE BOAT BRIGADE! I could jump overboard to preserve my integrity, but it might be a bit risky for the body.

Well, either we didn't get close enough to cause a disruption, or we just didn't get caught. But I will tell you, when the *Discovery* space shuttle thundered off the launchpad and rolled over our heads above the open waters of the Atlantic, I experienced a rush like no other. It was an unforgettable moment for me. I still break out in a sweat as I reflect back, or maybe it's because of the public confession of this writing. Nevertheless, the sight was phenomenal. The shuttle roared, and the booster rockets separated and made their descent back toward the Atlantic.

Why are there two boosters? It's simple. There is strength in partnership. Two are better than one.

The Benefits of Friendship

Your life will never have maximum impact without partnership. There is greater capacity, balance, strength, security, and satisfaction when you live in partnership with others.

So let's pause to consider four features of friendship Solomon highlights in his journal. No doubt he is onto something important in the search process. He captures his reflections in short, succinct statements concerning the essential role of relationships.

Friendship Increases Your Productivity

Solomon says that two people "get a better return for their labor" (Eccles. 4:9 NLT). He contrasts this partnership with the laborer he used as a case study in verse 8. This man worked like a dog to be the "top dog," only to discover that he had a "dog's life."

Long before business journals were flaunting the buzzword *synergy*, Solomon said when two work together, they increase their effectiveness. Partnership makes you more productive. Combine your energies and your effort, and you'll soon discover new power and potential.

Doing the job alone—as mentioned in an earlier chapter—is a primary cause for lack of productivity in our lives. Have you tried to begin a workout regimen, a diet, or a new discipline in your life alone? It doesn't take long for other people (or your own rumbling stomach) to convince you to lighten up, back off, or try later, does it?

On the other hand, a true friend is willing to walk, run, lift, diet, or start a new discipline with you. Friendship can make a world of difference. Even on days when you struggle—as I am today because of a seasonal weight-loss program—you can cheer one another on. In fact, while writing these words, I took a break to call Connie. We talked about how fun it would be to blow our diet by ordering a large pizza. But in the end, we agreed on Lean Cuisine. Clearly, this choice lacks the momentary pleasure of fresh pizza dough with warm cheese stretching from my teeth, but it does reflect a productive partnership.

Friendship Reduces Your Vulnerability

Solomon says, "For if they fall, one will lift up his companion. But woe to him who is alone when he falls, for he has no one to help him up" (Eccles. 4:10).

This was a vivid picture in the minds of travelers through the Middle East in Solomon's day. Rocky and treacherous trails wound through mountainous regions, and the potential for an accident or a fall could leave a lone traveler without any means of help. No cell phones to make a call. No GPS to find a location. The traveler was isolated and alone. For this reason, Solomon emphasized the need for a traveling partner.

We need friends who can help us and provide strength in times of weakness, so don't travel alone.

Several years ago while living in South Florida, there was a tremendous initiative by the Palm Beach County Sheriff's Department to gather used cell phones for distribution to senior adults. Because so many moved to this area in retirement years and lived alone, there was a need to provide communication in a crisis situation. The goal was to ensure that no one would fall without access to a friend by phone.

Life is full of treacherous pathways. The potential for a fall is great. We need friends who can help us and provide strength in times of weakness, so don't travel alone.

Friendship Provides Security

Note the picture in Solomon's words: "If two lie down together, they will keep warm" (Eccles. 4:11). It is easy in our visually overexposed world to see this through a sensual lens. But the reality is that there is warmth in togetherness.

Travelers in Solomon's day were often openly exposed to the elements. Shared body warmth—huddling under cover—would prevent the exposure that threatened to cause the travelers to freeze to death.

Crowds create heat. We all get warm in a room without adequate ventilation. We share heat in a cold bed. And we experience the cover of another's care through the security in friendship. Don't miss this. Two have the ability to keep one from being overexposed. Covering brings security. You cannot self-generate the necessary "heat" of affirmation, encouragement, and support that is gained from true friendship.

The Swedes have a saying: "Shared joy is a doubled joy. Shared sorrow is a half sorrow."

Friendship Provides Safety

Finally, Solomon says, "Though one may be overpowered by another, two can withstand him" (Eccles. 4:12). There is safety in numbers. You need a friend fighting for you when others or obstacles form to fight against you. Two make a ready defense. We all need someone to watch our blind side and backside. Why? Attacks come in swift and sudden ways. A friend will not leave you without defense.

I love the words of nineteenth-century poet Charles C. Colton: "The firmest friendships have been formed in mutual adversity, as iron is most strongly united by the fiercest flame."

You cannot self-generate the necessary "heat" of affirmation, encouragement, and support that is gained from true friendship.

Solomon closes this section of thought with these words: "A threefold cord is not quickly broken" (Eccles. 4:12). If having one friend is good, then having two friends is better. With close friends, you are safe. You are secure. You have strength if you have the friendship factor at work in your life.

Bible scholars are quick to point out that this progression from one . . . two . . . three is reflective of how Hebrew poetry completes a thought or idea, as we saw in our discussion of Hebrew parallelism in chapter 3. A third party adds to the strength, security, and safety of the friendship factor.

When my daughter, Liz, was a little girl, I once commented on her beautiful braids. I later learned that what appeared to be just two strands of hair woven together were, in fact, three. It takes three to make a braid. It's the unseen strand that gives the braid its security and strength.

Christians understand this in the spiritual dimension when it comes to friendships. God is the completer of the threefold cord that builds, binds, and blesses human relationships.

God is the completer of the threefold cord that builds, binds, and blesses human relationships.

There is strength when your life is woven together with others. There is security and safety when a marriage or friendship is woven together with God. Solomon's message is clear: You need friendships and partnerships in your search for satisfaction. Life is about relationships. Relationships impact the quality of your life.

Solomon wrote, "There is a friend who sticks closer than a brother" (Prov. 18:24). I pray that you are blessed to discover and experience the friendship factor in your life. As someone has said, "After a friendship with God, a friend's affection is the greatest treasure here below."

LifeNotes

chapter 7

the friendship factor

Relationships are a vital part of everyone's search process.

Consider the Value of a Partner

"Two are better than one, because they have a good reward for their labor. For if they fall, one will lift up his companion. But woe to him who is alone when he falls, for he has no one to help him up. Again, if two lie down together, they will keep warm; but how can one be warm alone? Though one may be overpowered by another, two can withstand him. And a threefold cord is not quickly broken" (Eccles. 4:9–12).

The Benefits of Friendship

Your life will never have maximum impact without part- nership. There is greater capacity, balance, strength, security, and satisfaction when you live in partnership with others.

Friendship Increases Your Productivity

When two work together, they increase their effectiveness. Partnership makes you more productive.

Friendship Reduces Your Vulnerability

Life is full of treacherous pathways. The potential for a fall is great. We need friends who can help us and provide strength in times of weakness.

Friendship Provides Security

You cannot self-generate the necessary "heat" of affirmation, encouragement, and support that is gained from true friendship.

Friendship Provides Safety

We all need someone to guard our blind side and our backside.

There is strength when your life is woven together with others. You need friendships and partnerships in your search for satisfaction.

The dumbest people I know
are the ones who know it all.

–MALCOLM FORBES, PUBLISHER OF *Forbes* MAGAZINE

chapter 8

random reflections

Ecclesiastes 5-8

People do some really dumb things. Last week, I read about two men traveling on Interstate 380 whose travel was abruptly interrupted when the hood of their car popped open and covered the windshield. What did they do? What would you do?

Here's the rest of the story: "Instead of pulling over to fix the problem, the men stuck their heads out the windows so they could see and kept moving in excess of 55 mph."

Sheriff's deputies got a firsthand look at the men and their blind joy ride and pulled them over. Imagine that conversation: "Sir, did you notice that your hood was open and this might contribute to dangerous driving conditions?"

The result was that the two men were arrested "on suspicion of driving under suspension and no proof of insurance." The sheriff's final comment was, "It's a little bit hard to drive with the hood of the car laid over the window."[1]

Is that an understatement?

Only the foolish would increase their speed, having lost sight of their way. But people do it every day. Not on the highway but on the journey of life.

For this reason, Solomon warns against pursuing a life that proves to be nothing more than motion and existence rather than content and consequence.

Only the foolish would increase their speed, having lost sight of their way.

In chapters 5 through 8 of his journal in Ecclesiastes, Solomon offers some seemingly random reflections. He circles back through some earlier observations and sketches additional thoughts for our consideration and reflection.

We all do this from time to time. We have thoughts and reflections we rehearse, revisit, and recycle over and over again. We do this with the hope that we will discover a breakthrough in understanding or that we will firm up a concept we don't want to forget.

As we approach this portion of Solomon's journal, we read a series of thoughts and reflections that seems somewhat random. It is as if he takes time to review the insights he has recorded thus far and reflects on what must not be forgotten along the way.

Let's take a few minutes to review some important insights as Solomon charts the course of his own search.

Recognize This: God Is Serious Subject Matter

Solomon writes, "Guard your steps when you go to the house of God. Go near to listen rather than to offer the sacrifice of fools, who do not know that they do wrong. Do not be quick with your mouth, do not be hasty in your heart to utter anything before God. God is in heaven and you are on earth, so let your words be few. . . . Do not let your mouth lead you into sin. . . . Much dreaming and many words are meaningless. Therefore stand in awe of God" (Eccles. 5:1–2, 6–7 NIV).

For many, says Solomon, religion is an accessory in an over-crowded life. What they practice they do by pretense. They go through time-honored routines of attendance, service, and verbal sacrifice. Yet in the end, more is said than done.

Solomon reminds the reader that the things of God are not trivial pursuits, nor does God tolerate hypocritical ritual. God sees. God knows. God weighs the minds and hearts of all people. Thinking rightly about God is the foundational issue in our life search.

Yet herein lies the problem. Most people have enough religion to make themselves miserable and to make God sick. So much of what goes on is religion on parade.

Did you know the Bible is not big on religion? The Bible places great emphasis on faith and responding to God as He is revealed in the Scripture. In contrast, religion is a "do-it-yourself" endeavor attempting to gain right standing with God by establishing the merit of your own goodness. Such religious pursuit has done more to condemn than change anyone in the world.

Most people have enough religion to make themselves miserable and to make God sick.

Solomon is strong and severe in his observation. When we approach God, we must not come convinced of our ability to live up to a standard that is pleasing to God. Instead, Solomon challenges us to "guard [our] steps," to "not be hasty," and to "stand in awe of God." Is Solomon trying to scare us? No. He is underscoring the need for us to approach God on God's terms and not our own. We must be clear in our understanding of what God expects rather than establishing our own self-made religion.

If we look for answers in religion while living in search mode, religion won't satisfy us. It won't satisfy God.

In recent years, a chain of stores called Build-A-Bear Workshops has populated malls across America. Build-A-Bear is a revolutionary concept in the toy-making industry and a highly popular activity for kids of all ages. The concept is creative, cute, and cuddly. At these stores, you can create a bear of your own design and imagination. You can choose the color, size, and themed outerwear. You can even put a recorded message in your bear so that when squeezed in the right way, the bear speaks on cue.

However, when we move from the workshops in the mall to places of worship, the "build-a-faith" concept does not translate. We do not pick and choose our own standards of righteousness, justice, and acceptability before God. There is no such thing as "personal assembly" or "spiritual accessory" religion.

Solomon distances himself from every self-directed religious impulse and reminds us that in life we must take God seriously. And this is the heart of the problem: we can take ourselves too seriously and fail to take God seriously enough.

God is serious subject matter.

Remember This: Money Is Fool's Gold for the Heart

How could Solomon say it any clearer? "Those who love money will never have enough" (Eccles. 5:10 NLT). Yet day after day, we pursue purchases in our search to add significance to our lives and take away the dissatisfaction of our souls.

Throughout Ecclesiastes 5 and 6, Solomon processes thoughts he captured earlier in his journal. He expands his warning concerning the dangers of seeking satisfaction in riches. He reminds us that even if we get what we want in life, we may not want what we get.

Solomon highlights this thought when he says, "There is a grievous evil which I have seen under the sun: riches being hoarded by their owner to his hurt" (Eccles. 5:13 NASB). And again, "All a man's labor is for his mouth and yet the appetite is not satisfied" (Eccles. 6:7 NASB).

This is the heart of the problem: we can take ourselves too seriously and fail to take God seriously enough.

Here the concern has to do with guarding, protecting, and risking loss of all you work so hard to achieve. How foolish, says Solomon, to believe the lie that riches, wealth, and abundance will bring satisfaction!

In America, the pioneers saw this lie lived out to its darkest end during the Yukon Gold Rush of the late 1890s. The reports of what happened to the men and women who risked their lives to find fortune are sobering. As the rush began in the northern territories, people pressed toward a landmass once ridiculed as worthless and desolate at the time of its purchase by the U.S. secretary of state. However, when the cry of "Gold!" echoed from these harsh areas, thousands pressed through the passages of the region in search of fortune and satisfaction.

In less than two years, the rush was over. By mid-1897, it is estimated that nearly thirty thousand people made their way to Dawson City in Canada's Yukon Territory. Twenty-two million dollars' worth of gold was found in rivers and creeks throughout the region. But in the end, only a few hundred people retained their wealth for any length of time. Many risked everything. Few found reward. Most regretted a search that led to nowhere.

These words were found on the side of a building in Dawson City:

The Spell of the Yukon

I wanted the gold and I sought it
I scrabbled and mucked like a slave
Was it famine or scurvy I fought it
I hurled my youth into a grave
I wanted the gold and I got it
Came out with a fortune last fall
Yet somehow life's not what I thought it
And somehow gold isn't all[2]

Solomon said the same thing nearly two millennia ago. Yet today, many search feverishly to acquire more and more gold, only to personalize this epitaph with their energies and their lives.

For all of the "bling" it brings to the eye, money does not bring lasting satisfaction to the heart.

Remember, says Solomon, money is like fool's gold for the heart. For all of the "bling" it brings to the eye, money does not bring lasting satisfaction to the heart.

Don't get blinded by riches. They never satisfy.

Reflect on This: Life Is a Series of Trade-offs

In Ecclesiastes 7, Solomon challenges us to evaluate and consider what matters most in life. It's evident that a broad series of searches led Solomon to list some lessons he learned along the way.

Exposure and experience proved to be powerful instructors in the life of this great king.

While the thoughts captured in this section of the journal appear to be random, they are cumulative. Solomon gives us some substantial wisdom for life.

A part of true satisfaction is being a man or a woman of proven character.

Solomon begins to summarize things he learned and establishes a profile of things we need to know. For all of the indulgences and excesses Solomon experienced, he is resolute in his summary: "A good name is better than precious ointment, and the day of death than the day of one's birth" (Eccles. 7:1).

Character counts! Your name, your character, what people say about you at the end of your life are what matter. A part of true satisfaction is being a man or a woman of proven character. This is better by far.

Better is the key word throughout Ecclesiastes 7. Solomon challenges us to think by offering comparisons, and he highlights what is better. If you take time to read the entire chapter, you will discover many valuable lessons for life. In the end, seeking satisfaction in a good life with good decisions and good intentions will never be enough.

There is a curious close to all the wisdom and instruction found in Solomon's observations: "'Here is what I have found,' says the Preacher, 'adding one thing to the other to find out the reason, which my soul still seeks but I cannot find: one man among a thousand I have found, but a woman among all these I have not found. Truly, this only I have found; that God made man upright, but they have sought out many schemes'" (Eccles. 7:27–29).

People search in error. People live in vain. People trade the best of life for the worst. People are made for God's purpose, but people do stupid things under the sun. They don't know what it is they seek and are disappointed in their search for satisfaction. They seek satisfaction apart from the One who made them upright.

Let's summarize a few parting thoughts:

- Religion apart from a relationship with the true and living God is empty, even evil.
- Wealth for the sake of wealth is a want without satisfaction.
- Wisdom is a grand goal, but you will never be wise enough without God.

Through his cycling of thought and the random records of these pages, Solomon is nearing an end. But there is one other subject that cannot be avoided and must be addressed. Try as you may to deny, ignore, or escape it, this is the ultimate reality: you must face the "D" word.

random reflections

We all tend to recycle our thoughts. We hope that the process of repetition, review, and reflection yields insight and understanding overlooked before.

Ecclesiastes 5–8 recycles and reassesses insights Solomon has learned along the way.

Recognize This: God Is Serious Subject Matter

"Keep your foot [give your mind to what you are doing] when you go . . . to the house of God. For to draw near to hear and obey is better than to give the sacrifice of fools [carelessly, irreverently] too ignorant to know that they are doing evil. Be not rash with your mouth, and let not your heart be hasty to utter a word before God. For God is in heaven, and you are on earth; therefore let your words be few" (Eccles. 5:1–2 AMP).

Solomon warns those who attempt to treat religion as an accessory in an overcrowded life. You can't be casual about things that pertain to God.

You must approach God on His terms and not your own.

Remember This: Money Is Fool's Gold for the Heart

"He who loves silver will not be satisfied with silver, nor he who loves abundance with gain. This also is vanity [emptiness, falsity, and futility]!" (Eccles. 5:10 AMP).

Someone has said, "Money can buy you anything but happiness and take you anywhere but heaven."

Reflect on This: Life Is a Series of Trade-offs

"A good name is better than precious ointment, and the day of death than the day of one's birth" (Eccles. 7:1).

Better is the key word of Ecclesiastes 7. Solomon points toward a better way to live.

Don't make foolish trades with your life. Choose the way of wisdom.

I'm not afraid to die;
I just don't want to be there when it happens.

—WOODY ALLEN, WRITER, ACTOR, DIRECTOR

chapter 9

the "d" word

Ecclesiastes 9

A couple of years ago, summer travels took our family to Boston. Like other tourists in this cradle of American history, we traced the Freedom Trail through early meeting houses, churches, the home of Paul Revere, Bunker Hill, and, of course, the Old Granary Burying Ground. This cemetery is one of the oldest in America. It is estimated that some sixteen hundred people are buried in this tiny graveyard that today is swallowed in the heart of downtown Boston.

The notable thing about the Old Granary is that many of the early American patriots are buried there. When you enter the gates, your eye is drawn to the large central obelisk bearing the name "Franklin." This stone marks the graves of the parents and family of our beloved Benjamin. While Ben Franklin died and was buried in Philadelphia, the grave marker in the heart of Boston reminds us of his revolutionary roots. You also find gravestones with the names

Samuel Adams, John Hancock, Robert Treat Paine, and Boston's son, Paul Revere. There is even one grave marked Mary Elizabeth Goose, believed to be the famed Mother Goose.

I spent some time walking through this plot of ground, studying the epitaphs of patriots whose lives, ideals, and sacrifice shaped the history of America. I also read about men and women whose names were memorialized but not familiar to me. I wondered about their lives, their faith, their spouses, their children. I imagined the trail of tears that led families to this place so long ago and considered the strange familiarity I felt. Why? I am a pastor. I have walked to the graveside with many. I know the drama and the dirge of such an hour.

Death is both our terror and our instructor.

One epitaph was of particular interest to me: "Captain John DeCoster, died January 28, 1773, at age 26." Inscribed below were these words:

> Stop here my friend and cast an eye,
> as you are now so once was I,
> as I am now so you must be,
> prepare for death and follow me.

Spooky words? Harsh reflections? Tragic history? No. It is a reality we all must face and something we all fear. Death is both our terror and our instructor.

The Reality of Death

Death is not a subject I enjoy. Hardly a day passes when I am not touched by it. Most of us avoid any personal reference to the subject. Isn't it strange that we are fascinated by death on the one hand

and stalked by it on the other? The daily news, nightly entertainment, and regular reminders in the obituary draw us ever nearer. We hope to keep our distance, yet we find death's footprints along the path of life.

Solomon's words were equally sharp and piercing. "No one has power over the spirit to retain the spirit, and no one has power in the day of death" (Eccles. 8:8).

All of us face a same and sure outcome—someday, we will die.

Death is an "equal-opportunity employer." It is the equalizer of us all: rich, poor, young, old, educated, uneducated, talented, limited, prestigious, obscure. All of us face a same and sure outcome—someday, we will die.

In wisdom, Solomon writes: "All things come alike to all: one event happens to the righteous and the wicked; to the good, the clean, and the unclean; to him who sacrifices and him who does not sacrifice. As is the good, so is the sinner; he who takes an oath as he who fears an oath. This is an evil in all that is done under the sun: that one thing happens to all. . . . They live, and after that they go to the dead" (Eccles. 9:2–3).

You probably feel this chapter and subject are best handled with a "fast-forward" approach. But wait. I challenge you to stick it out.

Solomon's search did not omit any keywords or leave any core issues untouched. He addressed the ultimate "fear factor" for most of us. He took time to contemplate the crypt. He knew that wherever our search for satisfaction might take us, we would weigh our discovery in light of the shadowy figure cast by the final reality of death.

The ratio is staggering: one out of one person dies. This is not exactly motivational conversation. In fact, if you want to clear up any lingering conversation around the coffeepot or watercooler, just surface the subject of death. It won't take long for everyone to find something better to do.

However, death is the unavoidable, inescapable, ultimate variable in life. It is the proverbial elephant in the room of your existence day after day. You can try to distract yourself from awareness or deceive yourself into believing you can ignore it, but sometimes you just need to admit that there is an elephant-sized subject that needs a few minutes of your time.

Death is a keyword in the search bar of life. When you see all you see, get all you get, do all you do, go where you go, and know all you know, you have to ask, "What does it matter in the end?"

How do you handle the subject matter and significance of the subject of death? Hollywood glamorizes death through violence, drama, and music. Some communities even economize death with casket stores in strip malls, displaying banners that advertise "Cash and Carry" coffins. Imagine that! *Hey, I need to borrow your truck. I've got to go pick up a casket.* That will test the bonds of friendship.

Some businesses commercialize death with expensive vaults, monuments, and extravagant funeral services. Some privatize it with silence, solemnity, and solitude. Others specialize in the artistry of family urns, burials at sea, or services that let you exit in style.

Culturally, America is engaged in a battle over how far we will go in efforts to legalize death with abortion on demand, euthanasia, and physician-assisted suicide. Each issue reflects a devaluation of the sanctity of human life and attempts to empower courts and individuals with "rights" of greater determinism in the matter of death. I am convinced our forefathers never would have dreamed of issues of such moral and legal magnitude being included in the rights guaranteed by our Constitution.

All this and much more can be included in a discussion on the subject of death, but most important, we need to personalize the issue of death. That is, each of us must acknowledge, accept, and address the reality of death as we plot and plan the course of life.

Death Shows Us How to Live

An awareness of and an understanding of our own face-off with death change how we view life under the sun.

On August 10, 1989, Dave Dravecky, a major-league pitcher for the San Francisco Giants, won the hearts of the American public and the entire world of baseball when he made a comeback following a severe surgery to remove a career-threatening cancer in his pitching arm.

Five days after his monumental comeback, the Giants were in Montreal, Canada. A loud crack, which sportswriters called "the pitch heard round the world," caused Dave to topple to the mound. In front of a packed stadium and worldwide television audience, he was placed on a stretcher and carried from the pitcher's mound to an awaiting ambulance. All his hopes and dreams of a comeback turned into a nightmare and fight for survival when he learned he again had to battle the aggressive growth of a life-threatening cancer in his pitching arm. Dave faced not only additional surgery but also the amputation of his left arm—his pitching arm.

Thankfully, this is not the end of the story. Dave survived and experienced a complete change in life, perspective, and focus as a result of what he and his wife, Jan, faced during those years.

Solomon urges us to face-off with death now so that we can get real about how to live life.

Jan once said, "When we face death, when we face the loss of loved ones, we desperately need a rock-solid hope. The thought this life is all there is—that we live and then die—is dreadful. When you realize how fragile life is, you search hard for truth. You have to know what is real. You need a hope beyond this life."[1]

This is Solomon's point in Ecclesiastes 9. It is not so much that you need to fear, tremble, or run at the reality of death. Solomon urges us to face off with death now so that we can get real about how to live life. Don't waste your life. Don't squander your opportunities. Don't overlook the best life has to offer.

"But for him who is joined to all the living there is hope, for a living dog is better than a dead lion" (Eccles. 9:4). Your life may not be like the "king of the jungle," but your life is precious and purposeful. Don't squander the only life you have. Don't let your search-mode living cause you to miss what life has to offer today.

Solomon is not writing about death as a fatalist; he writes as a realist. What's the bottom line of Solomon's journal entry? *Get real* about death and then *get on* with living a life that matters today.

It's time for us to move past the funeral home. But before you exit this passage concerning your most formidable foe, make some final arrangements.

Understand the Truth About Death

Be sure you understand death in light of ultimate truth. Some people think death is only a *temporary transition*, a place to settle the unfinished business of earth. Others view death as a struggle toward settlement and release, with the hope and prayers for the dead to be released into some ultimate rest. The writings of Solomon and the rest of the Scriptures don't support this post-life, transitory resolution.

Possibly you see death as a *recycling reincarnation*. Eastern mysticism and religions have long viewed life as an unbroken stream of energy and essence in formation and renewal. Life is one force with many expressions. This concept presents all life in the process of a "celestial recycling program." But again, this notion is far from the clear and specific instruction of the Bible. In fact, in the face of all mystical musings on this subject, Scripture declares, "It is appointed for men to die once, but after this the judgment" (Heb. 9:27). This is

a New Testament reference written hundreds of years after the time
of Solomon, but it gives us the same "straight talk" we read about
in his journal.

Perhaps you see death as a *complete cessation*. Birth is a fluke, life
is a fate, and death is a finale. While simplified, this view is one of
complete and utter fatalism. The curtain falls and it's over. Nature
moves on, and your life is but a blip on the screen of time.

For this reason, Solomon framed his thoughts concerning life
when he wrote, "He [God] has planted eternity in the human heart"
(Eccles. 3:11 NLT). Solomon's view of death is a date with destiny.
Death moves you from life under the sun to what lies beyond. This is
the ultimate purpose of your existence and the final destiny of your
experience. However, there remains one indispensable and undeniable
reality concerning what lies ahead. There is destiny in eternity, but
this destiny is not equal for all. One is a fearful destiny of judgment;
the other is a promise found in the Word of God.

Death Is the Penalty of Sin

We all need to get a grip on the real meaning of death before the
grim reaper's hand touches our lives. The essential is this: death is
the *penalty of sin*. Let's take a moment to trace this teaching in the
larger context of the Bible. Take a brisk walk from the Garden of
Eden to the golden age of Rome. Don't miss these steps.

In the Garden of Eden, God told Adam and Eve, "Of the tree of
the knowledge of good and evil you shall not eat, for in the day that
you eat of it you shall surely die" (Gen. 2:17). Their disobedience
caused the mark of sin to be branded on every human ever born. As
the apostle Paul explains in his letter to the Romans, "Through one
man [Adam] sin entered the world, and death through sin, and thus
death spread to all men, because all sinned" (Rom. 5:12). In other
words, death is the penalty every human has to pay for the sin he or
she inherited at birth. Paul makes it clear: "The wages of sin is
death" (Rom. 6:23).

Death Is Our Enemy

Scripture also presents death as our *enemy*. The apostle Paul says, "The last enemy that will be destroyed is death" (1 Cor. 15:26). This verse has helped me time and time again when I have been faced with unexplained tragedy, injury, and loss. Death is our enemy.

Death Is the Pathway into Eternity

Next, the Bible presents death as the *pathway into eternity*. From his early days as a shepherd boy, David, Solomon's father, captured this thought in the familiar words of Psalm 23: "Though I walk through the valley of the shadow of death, I will fear no evil; for You are with me" (v. 4). In this familiar psalm, David portrays death as a shadowed pathway through a dark valley that leads from here to eternity.

Death Is Defeated in the Victory of Jesus Christ

Finally, the Bible views death in light of the *victory of Jesus Christ*. This is the fundamental tenet of the Christian faith. What Paul says in Romans 6:23 is true: "The wages of sin is death." But the rest of the verse gives the good news: "but the gift of God is eternal life in Christ Jesus our Lord." And although we were branded by the mark of Adam's sin, Jesus Christ paid the penalty of death for us, so that we could be forgiven and our sin taken away. As Paul said, "As by one man's [Adam's] disobedience many were made sinners, so also by one Man's [Jesus's] obedience many will be made righteous" (Rom. 5:19).

Christ lived, Christ died, Christ rose again on the third day. He tasted death for you (Heb. 2:9) that you might not fear death with Him.

So what about you? Are you still trapped in fear of death's dark penalty, or have you been freed to celebrate the victory of Jesus Christ? If you have placed your faith in Christ, you no longer have to be afraid of the "D" word. In fact, you can say with the apostle Paul, "Death is swallowed up in victory" (1 Cor. 15:54).

the "d" word

We are fascinated by death yet stalked by it every day. We hope to keep our distance, yet we find death's footprints along the path of life.

"No one has power in the day of death. There is no release from that war, and wickedness will not deliver those who are given to it" (Eccles. 8:8).

The Reality of Death

All of us face a same and sure outcome—someday, we will die.

"All things come alike to all: one event happens to the righteous and the wicked; to the good, the clean, and the unclean; to him who sacrifices and him who does not sacrifice. As is the good, so is the sinner; he who takes an oath as he who fears an oath. For a living dog is better than a dead lion" (Eccles. 9:2, 4).

We have no choice: *Death* is a keyword in the search bar of life.

Death Shows Us How to Live

An awareness and under-standing of your own face-off with death changes how you view life under the sun.

Solomon did not write about death as a fatalist but as a realist. He urges us to face off with death now so that we can get real about how to live life.

Get real about death and then *get on* with living a life that matters today.

Understand the Truth About Death

What is the view of death found in Scripture?

- Death is the penalty of sin.
- Death is our enemy.
- Death is the pathway into eternity.
- Death is defeated in the victory of Jesus Christ.

Enjoy the little things, for one day you may look back and realize they were the big things.

—ROBERT BRAULT, AUTHOR

simple pleasures

Ecclesiastes 9

I start each day with a hot cup of coffee. While I make frequent stops at Starbucks during any given week, my mornings usually begin with a cup of Dunkin' Donuts coffee brewed at home, served with half-and-half and three packs of Equal or Splenda. It's one smooth concoction!

This experience is also enhanced by one of today's greatest modern marvels: an automatic, self-timed coffeemaker. Most mornings I hear the gurgling brew as it echoes from the kitchen between 5:15 and 5:30 a.m. The first order of business at that early hour is figuring out who will fetch the first cup. In our house, "love is fixin' the coffee." I try, but it is always a better cup when Connie delivers. I know what you're thinking. *He lies there and acts like he doesn't hear the coffee or the alarm and makes his poor wife serve him.* Wrong! Although I do have my share of pampered mornings, I am up to the challenge also. There are many mornings when I stumble from the stupor of my sleep to the kitchen and pour a hot cup of joe for both Connie and me.

After coffee, Connie and I catch up on the morning news head-lines and talk about the events of the day. Then we hit the street for our morning walk. Typically we walk for about thirty minutes with Riley, our "trainer." Riley is a "Scocker"—a Scottish terrier and cocker spaniel mix—that we got from the pound. Riley is jet black with a few gray highlights in his bushy eyebrows and a bright pink tongue that hangs to the side when he pants. If it weren't for Riley's morn-ing exuberance, I fear Connie and I would bypass the walk in our routine and leap into the day. However, Riley's influence is good for our health. He is also the best dog we have ever had.

I have discovered that for all of the rigors and demands I meet in my daily schedule, my day goes better and my life is fuller when I follow this simple start-up routine. The coffee, the time with Connie, and our morning walks are simple pleasures that add so much to the quality of my life. In fact, I have found that no matter where we go or what we do, we enjoy our coffee talk and walk.

I share this with you for one simple reason. Having tackled the ominous subject of death, Solomon makes a sudden shift in his focus toward the simple pleasures of daily life. It's as if Solomon brewed a fresh cup of coffee and moved beyond the heavy subject matter of death to a fresh take on life.

In his translation of this passage, Eugene Peterson provides expression to this sudden outburst and emphasizes the change in Solomon's tone:

Seize life! Eat bread with gusto, drink wine with a robust heart. Oh yes—God takes pleasure in *your* pleasure! Dress festively every morning. Don't skimp on colors and scarves. Relish life with the spouse you love each and every day of your precarious life. Each day is God's gift. It's all you get in exchange for the hard work of staying alive. Make the most of each one! Whatever turns up, grab it and do it. And heartily! This is your last and only chance at it, for there's neither work to do nor thoughts to think in the company of the dead, where you're most certainly headed. (Eccles. 9:7–10 MSG)

The reality of death should not discourage living; the awareness of death should increase our value and appreciation of each day we have. It is the simple things in life that matter: The fresh dew of each new morning. The ability to enjoy a great meal. The opportunity to dress for the occasion. The time you spend with your mate. The love you share with friends. The work you do and the life you live should give you simple pleasure.

In a world where things are bigger, better, faster, and newer, we need to remember that much of what makes life really matter are the simple things.

In a world where things are bigger, better, faster, and newer, we need to remember that much of what makes life really matter are the simple things. Solomon understood this. The reality of death did not make Solomon treasure his riches; it made him treasure life! His insight in discovering daily contentment had much more to do with the simple things than the excess of riches and comforts associated with his throne of royalty. We too often overlook the importance of simple things.

While we must guard against basing our entire lives on Solomon's reflections in Ecclesiastes 9, this passage does give us simple insights for enriching life.

Thanksgiving Every Day

Eat and enjoy the goodness of food with friends! Eating is biblical. God gave us the capacity to eat and enjoy good food. Our sense of taste is not some accident of nature; it is a part of the unique and specific design of God. Eating is not a mere function for existence; it is an experience. (And some of us are very experienced!)

If you step all the way back to Genesis, the book of beginnings, you discover one of the first commands and provisions of God: "Of every tree of the garden you may freely eat; but of the tree of the knowledge of good and evil you shall not eat, for in the day that you eat of it you shall surely die" (Gen. 2:16–17). And we thought warning labels were something new!

God has some serious things to say about eating. The theological significance of this passage in Genesis is extreme, for it has much to do with the fall of the human race into sin. Human failure to heed this command and prohibition has resulted in exaggerated desire, lustful indulgence, spiritual isolation, and universal judgment.

Yet the command "You may freely eat" demonstrates the provision of God for your daily needs. In the New Testament, Jesus taught us to pray, "Give us this day our daily bread" (Matt. 6:11). Here in his journal, Solomon says to go and eat your bread with joy. Eating is a gracious provision for common enjoyment in life. Don't miss the value of a good meal; it is one of life's simple pleasures. And it is a cause for daily worship. Each time you stop to eat, pause and give thanks to God, "who gives us richly all things to enjoy" (1 Tim. 6:17).

God's gracious gifts of food and taste are among the simple pleasures of life.

Maybe you learned this simple prayer when you were young: "God is great, God is good, let us thank Him for our food. Amen." It is a prayer that teaches you about the nature of God and the importance of gratitude in life. It by far surpasses the prayer I learned as a teenager in Memphis: "Good food, good meat, good Lord, let's eat!"

Meals are great times to gather with friends and family. So many key life events center around meals. From holidays to anniversaries, birthdays to business deals, vacations to daily debriefings, meal-times matter. Solomon knew the importance of enjoying a good meal among loved ones, as he wrote, "Better is a dinner of herbs where love is, than a fatted calf with hatred" (Prov. 15:17).

Don't overlook this simple, vital insight: God's gracious gifts of food and taste are among the simple pleasures of life. His common grace is shared in every life as we partake of the joys of eating.

Before I leave the subject, you may be wondering about wine. Is Solomon saying for us to do our share of drinking? I am always amazed at how many times people take a simple reference and turn it into a platform for personal indulgence. Solomon described the folly of wine in Ecclesiastes 2:3: "I searched in my heart how to *gratify my flesh with wine*, while guarding my heart with wisdom, and how to lay hold on folly, till I might see what was good for the sons of men to do under heaven all the days of their lives" (emphasis added). Note the words I italicized in this verse. *Gratification* is not *satisfaction*. In fact, in the book of Proverbs, Solomon clearly stated his view on the use and abuse of wine: "Wine is a mocker, strong drink is a brawler, and whoever is led astray by it is not wise" (Prov. 20:1). How many marriages, families, and relationships have been impacted by the use and abuse of alcohol?

Such indulgence would never be met with God's approval. It is adverse to His nature and character. Solomon makes mention of God in this verse (Eccles. 9:7). By so doing, Solomon is not encouraging indulgence but rather challenging gratitude and thanksgiving for God's provision in the simple pleasures of life.

Positive Style

Solomon moves from the subject of dining to the matter of disposition. We should dress every morning in a way that expresses our intention to celebrate life! What attitude are you choosing to display today? "Let your garments always be white, and let your head lack no oil" (Eccles. 9:8).

Solomon's reflection and discussion on death did not lead him to the brink of depression and despair. You may think such morbid talk would lead to a gothic appearance of death: black attire, pale features, somber expression. No! Solomon says to get out your white garments and live each day in celebration. Let your dress express your delight to find the best in each day, not your anticipation of the worst. In fact, I love the way Eugene Petersen expresses this text: "Dress festively every morning. Don't skimp on colors and scarves" (Eccles. 9:8 MSG). Isn't that great?

> *Let your dress express your delight to find the best in each day,*
> *not your anticipation of the worst.*

The idea is that life is something to celebrate every day. When you get dressed, don't present a drab, depressed, and despairing disposition. Instead, dress in a way that says, "I'm going to enjoy life today to the fullest!" And if today should be your last day on planet Earth, don't look like you were dressed for the occasion. Dress to live, to laugh, and to celebrate the gift of this day. Outward dress can give expression to the attitude of the heart. In Proverbs, Solomon said, "A merry heart does good, like medicine" (Prov. 17:22).

Do you mind if I ask, "What color are *you* wearing today?"

Joyous Love

The next of Solomon's simple life instructions is quite specific: "Live joyfully with the wife whom you love" (Eccles. 9:9). Love your spouse, and you'll love your life! Marriage is a good and gracious blessing, a marvelous provision of God.

Marriage is taking a bad rap in our culture these days: housewives are desperate, husbands cheat, unmarried couples live together, and civil unions defy the biblical pattern and original intention of marriage. More and more, marriage is attacked and condemned.

Love your spouse and value him or her as a gift from God.

Solomon provides us with his God-given insight to the larger context of biblical marriage. Marriage is good. Marriage is a gift. Yet, sadly, many people have never seen a marriage that reflects biblical specifications. I appreciate the words of my friend and pastor, Jack Graham, who says,

> As Christians, our marriages are a testimony to the world if we are living as God planned. That's why when a Christian marriage melts down, it's a double tragedy. Not only are the people involved hurt by the breakup, but a testimony is lost because the world looks at the broken marriage and wonders what difference God makes. God intends marriage to communicate to the world His power to change lives through His grace and love.[1]

The Bible places high value and high standards on marriage. Specific instruction is given to men about how to maximize and maintain their marriages. A man is to honor, esteem, and value his wife. A woman is to respect, submit to, and bring honor to her husband.

Marriage is not a lifetime sentence but an opportunity to "do life together." I love how the Living Bible translates Solomon's challenge and encouragement to men: "Live happily with the woman you love through the fleeting days of life, for the wife God gives you is your best reward down here for all your earthly toil" (Eccles. 9:9).

Here's a straight-up challenge: love your spouse and value him or her as a gift from God. Solomon emphasizes this in Proverbs: "He who finds a wife finds a good thing, and obtains favor from the LORD" (Prov. 18:22).

Good marriages and healthy relationships are among the richest and best of life's simple pleasures.

Hard Work

Work is good and adds value to life. Most people spend the majority of their adult lives at work. Work is a necessity and provides a source of sanity. I have been amazed through the years to observe the attitudes and actions of those who have been "blessed" with the opportunity to retire young and be set for life. The only problem is they don't know what to do with their lives after they've retired. Having enough is never enough. We all need something to do.

I have heard it said that everyone needs three things in life: something to believe in, someone to love, and something to do. Work gives us something to do that brings purpose and completion to our days.

Like you, I often struggle to find days when I don't have anything to do. But when I finally find time to do nothing, I immediately start thinking of something that needs to be done. Now before you psychoanalyze my compulsive disorders, understand that I do enjoy downtime. But I think I am in good company when I want all of my time to count.

Not long ago, I had several free hours to do whatever I wanted.

My first impulse was to drive home and unwind in front of the television. However, as I made my way through my garage to the back door, I discovered an unopened box in the corner containing a new file cabinet. As I reached for the doorknob, the words "Assembly Required" caught my attention. To be honest, it wasn't a new delivery. It had been sitting there for over a month. You know the rest. It was time to go to work! Like most of my assembly purchases, I had the promise of simple assembly with all parts and tools included. *Yeah, right!* I uncovered a mass of sorted parts, insufficiently described in oversimplified instructions, along with a sole, inadequate tool. I found myself faced with a challenge to my manhood and postgraduate education as I questioned whether I was capable of complying with the instructions.

Simple pleasures remind us how good life can be.

However, at the end of the day, I positioned a newly assembled file cabinet not far from where I write today. The assembly proved challenging, but I found fulfillment in knowing I added value to the day by finishing a job at hand.

We all need to experience the output of effort and moments of accomplishment. Whether you work outside the home or dedicate your time to raising your children and managing your household, work is a necessary part of your total well-being. That is why Solomon wrote, "Whatever your hand finds to do, do it with your might" (Eccles. 9:10). Despite its stresses and challenges, work is a simple pleasure of life—the final one that Solomon highlights in his journal as he compresses his thoughts concerning life before death.

Several days ago, I received a card in the mail from my editor. Thankfully, the card wasn't a friendly reminder like those received from the library stating a book is overdue. This was a note of encouragement. Her card bore the image of a cup of coffee with the words, "Simple pleasures remind us how good life can be."

I am grateful for a postcard cup of coffee and a few inspirational words!

LifeNotes

chapter 10

simple pleasures

Life is fragile. Death is sure. Learn to enjoy the little things. The reality of death should not discourage living; the awareness of death should increase our value and appreciation of each day we have.

Thanksgiving Every Day

"Seize life! Eat bread with gusto, drink wine with a robust heart. Oh yes—God takes pleasure in *your* pleasure!" (Eccles. 9:7 MSG).

Eat and enjoy the goodness of food with friends.

Positive Style

"Dress festively every morning. Don't skimp on colors and scarves" (Eccles. 9:8 MSG).

Dress every morning to express your intent to live and celebrate life.

Joyous Love

"Relish life with the spouse you love each and every day of your precarious life. Each day is God's gift" (Eccles. 9:9 MSG).

Love your spouse, and you will love the life you live.

Hard Work

"Whatever your hand finds to do, do it with your might" (Eccles. 9:10).

Work is good and adds value to life.

Simple pleasures remind us how good life can be.

Expectations improperly indulged must end in disappointment.

—SAMUEL JOHNSON, LETTER, JUNE 8, 1762

chapter 11

when life seems unfair

Ecclesiastes 9

Arriving at the airport early enough to get through check-in and security in time to make a flight has become a modern art. I recently heard about a woman who, having maneuvered through the single-file portal of entry to her gate, paused to pick up a snack—chocolate-covered cookies and a hot cup of coffee.

She looked for a speaker where she could monitor the boarding call and found a seat with a small table between herself and another waiting passenger, a man who appeared fully engrossed in the *USA Today* sports section. Unloading the coffee, carry-on bags, and purse from her arms, she paused to retrieve the latest edition of *People* magazine and settled in to enjoy the coffee and cookies before the call to board.

What happened next was beyond belief. She unwrapped the package of cookies, took out the first of her newfound indulgences, and began reading her magazine. The man with the newspaper next to her simply reached over, pulled the cookies to his side of the table, and proceeded to eat a cookie without any apparent consideration for the woman.

Her frustration and discomfort with the situation began to escalate. She tried to focus on her magazine and ignore what had happened. But then she reached for another cookie, and within a moment he, too, reached to take another. She felt the heat of anger rising within.

Then it happened! She reached for the last cookie, but before her hand got beyond the edge of her magazine, his hand was on it. Her eyes cut from the magazine toward him. She glared with indignation. He calmly broke the cookie in half, offered her the other half, shrugged his shoulders, and gathered his things in response to the call to board.

Needless to say, this incredible turn of events left her with a split-second decision to either publicly blast the man for his heartless deed or maintain her composure and proceed to the gate. She chose the latter.

Our frustrations are most often the result of our own failure to come to terms with our attitudes.

The woman spent the next hour and a half seething at the nerve, the gall, the arrogance of a man who would act in such a self-indulging manner. She began to imagine a conversation between herself and this man, confronting him after the flight. The shock of the events that unfolded in the airport had left her speechless, but now she knew just what to do. *I'll write a note of protest and deliver it as we exit the plane,* she thought.

She reached into her bag for a pen and paper and, to her surprise, discovered her unopened sleeve of chocolate cookies. *The cookies on the table actually belonged to the man with the newspaper!* All the anger, frustration, and energy she had focused on her inconsiderate traveling companion were turned back on herself. She had been the problem all along!

Life is often like that. We don't often eat other people's cookies, of course, but the real source of our dissatisfaction often comes from our own misconceptions about what is fair, not from the efforts of others to take advantage of us.

It is not until we shift our focus and change our perspective under the sun that we are able to come to terms with our own reality glitches. Most of the frustrations and exasperations in life are not the fault of God letting us down, others "stealing our cookies," or even our circumstances being worse than our neighbor's. Our frustrations are most often the result of our own failure to come to terms with our attitudes.

Solomon made this insightful entry in his journal:

I returned and saw under the sun that—the race is not to the swift, nor the battle to the strong, nor bread to the wise, nor riches to men of understanding, nor favor to men of skill; but time and chance happen to them all. For man also does not know his time: like fish taken in a cruel net, like birds caught in a snare, so the sons of men are snared in an evil time, when it falls suddenly upon them (Eccles. 9:11–12).

Life is often traveled on uneven pavement. It has an unavoidable outcome for all. It has some unpredictable challenges. And life brings some unexplained surprises. None of us is immune to tough times or hard roads. The key is how we will navigate the inequities, the misjudgments, and the disappointments. Why? Because life so often seems unfair.

Life Seems Unfair Because of an
Unavoidable Outcome

You can't predict hard times or rough places when you face delays and meet repair crews along the way. Plan all you want and do what you can, but struggles in life are inevitable.

As you read these words today, you are traveling on one of three life pathways. Maybe today you are traveling on the road called "Trouble." It is a rough ride for sure, with potholes, flooded curbs, and pounding rains. Storms have overshadowed the progress of your dreams and designs. The pouring rains, adverse winds, and changing conditions have overwhelmed you. Your thoughts are focused on survival. Are you on the hard road today?

Maybe you are nearing the end of "Trouble" and turning on a new highway called "Hope." The clouds and storms that engulfed you are parting. Encouraging rays of hope are shining through. You are ready to embrace hope with gratitude and to enjoy the next few miles of life's journey.

But then there are those on the street called "Steady," which—I hate to say—will soon merge onto the road called "Trouble." They, too, will face the challenges and struggles common to all who journey there.

We all have this in common: we struggle with the fairness of life.

And so it is. Every day of your life, you are either in trouble, coming out of trouble, or going into trouble. This is the pattern of life under the sun. We can't change this reality, but we can choose the attitude and perspective we will embrace along the journey.

Solomon observed that life is often unfair. If I could emphasize the positive and negative aspects of Solomon's words in his journal, I would challenge you to consider this: "The race is not [always] to the swift, nor the battle [only] to the strong, nor bread [specifically] for the wise, nor riches [exclusively] to men of understanding, nor favor [given] to men of skill (Eccles. 9:11). We all have this in common: we struggle with the fairness of life.

Life Seems Unfair Because of Unpredictable Challenges

"People can never predict when hard times might come. Like fish in a net or birds in a snare, people are often caught by sudden tragedy" (Eccles. 9:12 NLT).

Advantages. Obstacles. Opportunities. Disappointments. Possibilities. Limitations. Good and bad. We all share the infirmities and inequities in life. As Elvis once sang, "We're caught in a trap!" (Forgive me, but my Memphis roots have a way of surfacing along the way.)

So what does this mean?

Abilities Can Be Liabilities

Ability is not a defense in the day of trouble. Your abilities do not provide automatic access to satisfaction or assurance of success. One thing we can learn in the tough places of life is that we can't build the security or find the satisfaction of our lives in our abilities alone. Many talented and gifted people are miserable.

We all have a tendency to compare ourselves with others. We might think, *If only I had his personality or her looks . . . If I could think like that or talk like that . . . If I could sing, remember, communicate like . . . or whatever.* We assess, compare, envy, or imitate others. We begin to think that fairness has to do with gifts, talents, and skills that others possess and we don't. For those of you who may be slipping into this mind-set, let me remind you: many capable people fail.

Maybe you are a capable person and you have failed. You are disappointed and feel defeated. Remember, everyone struggles, no matter how strong, beautiful, smart, or rich they are. The issue is not what others have that you don't. Rather, the questions you should be asking are: "How will I address the challenges with my own unique abilities? What will I do with my struggles? How will I view the disappointments and the defeats of life? Can I use the unexpected delays and the interrupted plans as launchpads for future successes?"

Opportunities Are Not Guarantees

The second thing you must learn from Solomon's wise words is that opportunity cannot provide access to a life of satisfaction. Many of us have known great opportunity. Others feel regret for opportunities lost. Some have tasted opportunity with regularity through the privileges of friendship, education, or economic prosperity. Still, opportunity in and of itself is not a guarantee to a life of satisfaction. Though opportunity is what many point to as the "missing link" in their life journey, it is not the global link to a satisfied life.

Opportunity cannot provide access to a life of satisfaction.

Whenever I think of opportunity lost, I think of Mike Tyson. If ever a man was given an opportunity to achieve what most can only dream of in life, it was "Iron Mike" Tyson. His is a Cinderella story gone sour. For all of his hard work and brutal survival, Tyson's life has been overshadowed by opportunity lost. My heart goes out to him. When I see or hear of him, I pray for him. I find great tragedy in observing that a man who once held honor, riches, rewards, and fame is now held in the undesirable category of "has-been."

Adversity Is Not Altogether Disability

Finally, we observe that adversity cannot withhold our access to satisfaction or success. If speed, strength, wisdom, riches, and privilege are not golden keys to a satisfied life, then the hardships of life cannot and will not keep us from true satisfaction. It's a fact. Adversity cannot prevent us from enjoying deep and lasting satisfaction. Why? Because many times life's greatest achievements and joys come from those who seem to be the weakest, the most limited, and the most unlikely to succeed.

This is a vital, life-changing concept. Hardships, limitations, deficiencies, and troubles can create breakthroughs. Life isn't fair, but the challenges in life bring balance. And the inevitable outcome, the unexpected challenges, and the unexplained surprises can take us to a place where we can trade our expectations of fairness for expressions of faith.

While Life Seems Unfair, There Are Often Unexpected Surprises

Do you know the name Charlotte Elliott? Charlotte grew up in a Christian home and desired to live a life that would please God and bless others. Yet she struggled on the road called "Trouble." As a child, she faced challenge, disease, and disability that left her confined to a wheelchair for life. Day after day, Charlotte felt like a prisoner in her own body and a captive in her own home.

Charlotte's brother grew up in this same home. At a young age, he felt called to be a pastor. He progressed in leadership and prominence, and he led a large church while Charlotte was left to a life of limitations and regrets. She struggled with overwhelming feelings of depression and defeat.

On one of her low days, her pastor stopped in for a visit. He took time to talk and pray with her, and Charlotte poured out to him the frustration and bitterness of her heart. She said, "I hate my life! My life is of no count. How could God ever use me?" Her wise pastor said that she needed to stop focusing on her limitations and to give herself just as she was to God. Charlotte took his words of encouragement to heart. She prayed about God's plan for her life and how she could find a way to honor God and help others.

From that day forward, Charlotte viewed her life and faith differently. Fourteen years later, she wrote a poem that was put to the music of William Bradbury:

> Just as I am, without one plea,
> But that Thy blood was shed for me,
> And that Thou bidst me come to Thee,
> O Lamb of God, I come, I come.

Whether you have a strong religious background or not, you probably have heard this hymn. It has been the music of invitation and decision for every Billy Graham crusade since 1949. There was never an hour of decision when Cliff Barrows failed to lead the choir to sing "Just as I Am," a song penned by a girl who struggled with her disabilities yet was used by God to touch lives around the world.

Millions have heard these compelling lyrics and walked forward in stadiums, coliseums, tents, and arenas as the Graham team preached a message of hope and challenged people to respond—just as they are—to God. Charlotte's brother once said, "In the course of a long ministry, I hope I have been permitted to see some of the fruit of my labor, but I feel far more has been done by a single hymn of my sister's: 'Just as I Am.'"[1]

Life isn't fair. It's a fact. But the lack of fairness cannot keep you from discovering true satisfaction. Like Charlotte, you may need to come to God and say, "Lord, I am disheartened, dissatisfied, and disappointed. But I come to you. I know satisfaction will never be found in fairness, only in faith."

when life seems unfair

Our frustrations are most often the result of our own failure to come to terms with our attitudes. The key is how we will navigate the inequities, the misjudgments, and the disappointments.

Life Seems Unfair Because of an Unavoidable Outcome

All people are on one of three roads:

1. Trouble—in trouble
2. Hope—coming out of trouble
3. Steady—going into trouble

Life Seems Unfair Because of Unpredictable Challenges

"I took another walk around the neighborhood and realized that on this earth as it is—the race is not always to the swift, nor the battle to the strong, nor satisfaction to the wise, nor riches to the smart, nor grace to the learned. Sooner or later bad luck hits us all" (Eccles. 9:11 MSG).

• Abilities can be liabilities.
• Opportunities are not guarantees.
• Adversity is not altogether disability.

While Life Seems Unfair, There Are Often Unexpected Surprises

Life isn't fair. It's a fact. But the lack of fairness cannot keep you from discovering true satisfaction.

A childhood illness left Charlotte Elliott an invalid. She became bitter until her pastor encouraged her to give herself, just as she was, to God. After this conversation, she penned the words to "Just as I Am," which has been sung at every Billy Graham crusade around the world.

It is amazing what can happen when we give our limitations to God!

Life is like a box of chocolates; you never know what you're gonna get.

—Winston Groom, *Forrest Gump*, 1986

chapter 12

wisdom's sampler

Ecclesiastes 10

In 1842 Stephen F. Whitman opened a "confection and fruiterer shop" in Philadelphia. Whitman's dream was to create an American brand of chocolate candy that would compete with that of the fine French candy makers of his day. Today many people celebrate holidays and special occasions with Whitman chocolates packaged in the traditional trademarked box.

The most common association we have with Stephen Whitman's candies is the much-loved and well-known Whitman's Sampler. It is estimated that one Whitman's Sampler box is sold every 1.5 seconds. The Sampler is affectionately admired because of its mixture of darks and lights, nuts and creams. You get a little bit of everything when you get a Whitman's Sampler.[1]

Sample the Wisdom for Living

In many ways, the wisdom found in chapter 10 of Solomon's journal creates for us a "Wisdom's Sampler." Solomon writes a series of life lessons so we can "taste" the value of wisdom in daily life. He begins, "Dead flies [nothing covered in chocolate here] make a perfumer's oil stink" (Eccles. 10:1 NASB).

The thrust of Ecclesiastes 10 is a contrast between wisdom and foolishness. In the "Wisdom's Sampler," Solomon links dead flies, deep pits, dull axes, snake charmers, and birds in an assortment of pivotal insights. Let's examine a few of Solomon's contrasts and comparisons. Do you remember the background of Hebrew parallelism given in chapter 3? You may find it helpful as you reflect on these words:

> Dead flies putrefy the perfumer's ointment, and cause it to give off a foul odor; so does a little folly to one respected for wisdom and honor. A wise man's heart is at his right hand, but a fool's heart at his left. Even when a fool walks along the way, he lacks wisdom, and he shows everyone that he is a fool. If the spirit of the ruler rises against you, do not leave your post; for conciliation pacifies great offenses. There is an evil I have seen under the sun, as an error proceeding from the ruler: folly is set in great dignity, while the rich sit in a lowly place. I have seen servants on horses, while princes walk on the ground like servants. (Eccles. 10:1–7)

Maybe you are thinking, *What does this have to do with wisdom? Is it some Middle Eastern riddle or mystical imagery?* No. It is a way of presenting a challenge of wisdom in word pictures that were practical and compelling to people in Solomon's day. Let's see if we can learn a few things from Solomon's words.

The Truth About Corrupting Influences

It doesn't take an extreme sense of imagination to understand how dead flies can ruin even the most exclusive and expensive of perfumes. In Solomon's day, fragrances were mixed with oil to make lotions much like the fragrant moisturizers we use today. The oil would soothe the skin, and the fragrance would refresh the body. But dead flies floating in a container would ruin the appearance and destroy the value of the perfume.

The purity of honor and value of virtue can be quickly tainted by foolish attitudes, decisions, and actions.

Solomon says this is the same effect of foolishness in life. The purity of honor and value of virtue can be quickly tainted by foolish attitudes, decisions, and actions. Don't play the fool. If you do, you will trade the value of your life for disrespect.

Foolishness abounds in the human heart. In fact, the word "foolishness" or "folly" is repeated nine times in Ecclesiastes 10. It seems as though Solomon is coming to terms with the fact that much of our stirring, searching, and restless pursuit in life comes out of the folly of the human heart. There is something wrong deep within us. There is a virus latent in our hearts that surfaces in our every search for satisfaction.

You can destroy your character and reputation with one act of foolish behavior. Whether you are a commoner or a king, foolishness is unbecoming. The most important thing is not what people see in your public image but what is found deep within your heart. It won't be long until "dead flies" evidence their presence. And in time, they stink. For this reason, Solomon wisely wrote, "Watch over your heart with all diligence, for from it flow the springs of life" (Prov. 4:23 NASB).

No amount of affluence, intelligence, experience, or competence can provide sufficient fragrance to cover the enduring presence of "dead flies" in the heart. The dead flies speak of foolish inclinations, the denial of consequence, the presence of deceit, and the belief that you can ignore or hide from God. What is the way of the fool? We learn from Solomon's father, David, in Psalm 14:1: "The fool has said in his heart, 'There is no God.'"

The Truth About Careless Lifestyles

"He who digs a pit will fall into it, and whoever breaks through a wall will be bitten by a serpent. He who quarries stones may be hurt by them, and he who splits wood may be endangered by it. If the ax is dull, and one does not sharpen the edge, then he must use more strength; but wisdom brings success" (Eccles. 10:8–10).

When Solomon spoke of workers who dug deep pits and fell into them, he was referring to people who dive into a life experience or an endeavor and throw caution to the wind. It is the "pit" of our own doing.

Digging is hard work. Digging without caution is dangerous work. Many pursuits in life are destructive, and Solomon is saying that some choose the lifestyles of fools. They dig to find satisfaction, only to fall into the pit of their own desire. They break through barriers of structure only to be bitten by serpents. They burrow into stones of protection only to experience the collapse of bedrock belief. They split the logs of life only to discover the injury of such splintered living.

You can't outwit, outlast, or outsmart God.

You can't outwit, outlast, or outsmart God. You won't survive. Instead, learn that if your ax is dull from use, you need to sharpen the blade. Wisdom will put an edge of effectiveness on the dullness of a life lived in folly. For this reason Solomon exclaims, "Wisdom has the advantage of giving success" (Eccles. 10:10 NASB). Solomon is starting to wise up!

The Truth About Condemning Words

"A serpent may bite when it is not charmed; the babbler is no different. The words of a wise man's mouth are gracious, but the lips of a fool shall swallow him up; the words of his mouth begin with foolishness, and the end of his talk is raving madness. A fool also multiplies words" (Eccles. 10:11–14).

Snake charmers have always garnered the attention of others. We're fascinated by men who can look into the eyes of such a venomous foe and command its attention and response. But the reality is that no man can truly charm a snake. The unpredictable nature and the belying character of such a creature always leave us in harm's way.

No matter how much others may try to "charm" it, the tongue of a fool is venomous in the lives of those who stand near.

Such is the nature of an uncontrolled tongue. No matter how much others may try to "charm" it, the tongue of a fool is venomous in the lives of those who stand near.

In his commentary on Solomon's writings, Warren Wiersbe does an excellent job of identifying the toxic qualities of a foolish tongue. He mentions "destructive words" (10:12), "unreasonable words" (10:13), "uncontrolled words" (10:14), and "boastful words" (10:15).[2] How often is your speech marked by such words? What injury do you bring to God, to yourself, and to others because of an unguarded tongue?

Richard Strauss tells the story of the dangerous and scandalous impact of gossip in a small North Dakota community. A mother had not been well since the birth of her second baby, but everyone knew she did all she could to create an atmosphere of love in the home. The neighbors could see the young wife and their two small children greeting the father at the door each evening with hugs and kisses. In summer when the windows were open, they could hear the laughter and joyous fun coming from inside the house.

Then one day, a village gossip whispered that the man was being unfaithful to his wife, a story completely without basis. It was passed on by others and eventually came to the wife's ears. It was more than she could bear. One evening when her husband came home, no one met him at the door. There was a deathly silence in the air. His wife had taken her own life and those of her two children. He was overcome with grief. His innocence was proven to all, but the gossip's tongue had already done its work.

Death and life are in the power of the tongue. It is full of deadly poison. Though the results of your unchecked words may not be as drastic as in this case, you can do much damage and bring irreparable injury with the destructive nature of an unguarded tongue.

I share this story because it so clearly parallels the closing warning found in Solomon's wisdom in Ecclesiastes 10:20: "Furthermore, in your bedchamber do not curse a king, and in your sleeping rooms do not curse a rich man, for a bird of the heavens will carry the sound and the winged creature will make the matter known" (NASB).

Solomon's life search provides an assortment of life lessons that allows us to sample God's wisdom in a day when foolish living is indulged to excess.

LifeNotes

chapter 12

wisdom's sampler

In many ways, the wisdom found in chapter 10 of Solomon's journal creates for us a "Wisdom's Sampler." Solomon urges us to "taste" the value of wisdom in daily life.

Sample the Wisdom for Living

The thrust of Ecclesiastes 10 is a contrast between wisdom and foolishness.

The Truth About Corrupting Influences

"Dead flies putrefy the perfumer's ointment, and cause it to give off a foul odor; so does a little folly to one respected for wisdom and honor" (Eccles. 10:1).

You can destroy your character and reputation with one act of foolish behavior. No amount of positive fragrance can over-shadow a corrupting presence. Don't play the fool.

The Truth About Careless Lifestyles

"He who digs a pit will fall into it, and whoever breaks through a wall will be bitten by a serpent. He who quarries stones may be hurt by them, and he who splits wood may be endangered by it. If the ax is dull, and one does not sharpen the edge, then he must use more strength; but wisdom brings success" (Eccles. 10:8-10).

Solomon warns against people who dive into a life experience or an endeavor and throw caution to the wind. It is the "pit" of our own doing.

You can't outwit, outlast, or outsmart God. You won't survive.

The Truth About Condemning Words

"A serpent may bite when it is not charmed; the babbler is no different. The words of a wise man's mouth are gracious, but the lips of a fool shall swallow him up; the words of his mouth begin with foolishness, and the end of his talk is raving madness. A fool also multiplies words" (Eccles. 10:11-14).

No matter how much others may try to "charm" it, the tongue of a fool is venomous in the lives of those who stand near.

Solomon's life search provides an assortment of life lessons that allow us to sample God's wisdom in a day when foolish living is indulged to excess.

A little philosophy inclineth men's hearts to atheism; but depth in philosophy bringeth men's minds about to religion.

—SIR FRANCIS BACON, *Of Atheism*, 1607

chapter 13

a view from the bottom

Ecclesiastes 11

Bankruptcy. The word has become all too familiar amid stories of corporate failure and personal disaster in recent years. I remember the day I sat in a barber's chair getting a haircut and thumbing through a *Time* magazine. This particular edition featured the history-making growth and expansion of the Enron Corporation and touted the phenomenal impact of Enron's signature on the Houston skyline—a soaring new office tower complete with a ballpark and other "Enronized" features. At that time, no one knew that within six months of the publication of this article, this energy giant would plummet into Chapter 11 bankruptcy and create a domino effect for corporate America that would result in thousands of jobs and billions of dollars lost in the wake of Enron's financial upheaval and destruction.

Five Lessons from a Royal Bankruptcy

Solomon also had a "Chapter 11" end to his own life search. After he hit bottom, he surveyed the landscape of his life and concluded that his pursuits and assumptions only added to the frustration of a dissatisfied life. In his life journal, Solomon records a series of life discoveries relevant today to help you avoid the same empty endeavors. He offers five insights to help you move from vain existence to capture a new vision in the days to come.

"Cast your bread upon the waters" (Eccles. 11:1) is a phrase that has found its way from the pages of Solomon's ancient journal to conversations even today. It conveys the idea of taking risks. From this opening challenge, Solomon confronts the accepted thinking of this age and inspires us toward a fresh perspective in daily living.

Look at this list of life discoveries and consider their impact on our daily pursuits.

1. Satisfaction Is Found in Letting Go Rather Than Holding On

The idea that satisfaction is found by letting go is both upstart and upstream in a culture that thrives on acquisition and consumption. Driving the advertisements that bombard us each day is the subtle message that life consists of the things we possess; therefore, the more we get, the better off we will be, right? Wrong! Solomon declares that satisfaction is found not in getting but in giving.

Maybe you are thinking, *How did you get that idea out of soggy bread?* In the ancient world, commerce and travel were quite different from today. One common practice was loading seafaring vessels with grains from regions rich with fertile soils. Merchants took harvested crops and grains to sell at distant seaports. In return, the merchants brought back the profits and benefits of such trade to the farmers and merchants of their homeland.[1]

Of course, ancient farmers and merchants did not have the

advancements in travel, technology, and communication we often take for granted today. There were no "overnight" shipping options. Instead, every export came with the risk of catastrophe at sea or robbery. The entire season's crop—potentially a year's income—could be lost.

Note the second half of Ecclesiastes 11:1: "for you will find it after many days." Is Solomon talking about actual bread floating on the water? No. He is speaking to the weary seaman and, I might add, in terms that today's crowded and consumer-driven age will understand. Solomon is referring to a real and rewarding *return on investment*. I think *The Message* captures it best: "Be generous: Invest in acts of charity. Charity yields high returns" (Eccles. 11:1).

Life is not about getting; it is about giving.

Life is not about getting; it is about giving. When you risk loss to give, you can discover the greater gain of the return of gratitude. Getting makes you proud; giving makes you humble. When you give, you release. When you risk the loss of something of value, you gain the benefit of something far greater. Are you willing to challenge the popular notion that life is all about getting?

You can go through life thinking that everything revolves around who you are, what you do, and what you have. Yet somehow life remains off-center. Why? Because you may have believed the lie that life is about getting and that the acquisition of things is the avenue to satisfaction.

Solomon challenges this attitude. He found that to be generous in a world of greed is one step toward obtaining satisfaction in life. He urges us to give to others: "Give a serving to seven, and also to eight, for you do not know what evil will be on the earth" (Eccles. 11:2). Bible scholar Walt Kaiser wrote concerning this text, "Be liberal and generous to as many as you can and then some. Make as many friends as you can, for you never know when you yourself may need some assistance."[2]

Don't spend your life hoarding; greater satisfaction is found through release. Experience the thrill of giving!

2. Satisfaction Is Found in Our Commitments, Not Our Circumstances

I like the simple, straightforward challenge of the New Living Translation: "When the clouds are heavy, the rains come down. When a tree falls, whether south or north, there it lies. If you wait for perfect conditions, you will never get anything done" (Eccles. 11:3–4). If you always wait for fair conditions in life, there is much that simply will not get done. Dissatisfaction can come from focusing on circumstances rather than commitments.

Are you a perfectionist when it comes to the conditions of life? Do you want everything to be just right? Life is rarely that way. Even when I enjoy a perfectly beautiful day (sunny and 76 degrees) and I find a perfectly wonderful place (a pool overlooking the ocean), it's not long before I discover my dream of perfection can be ruined by a bee or a fly intent on invading my space.

Solomon paints two word pictures in this passage to display challenging life circumstances: clouds and trees. Clouds can appear out of nowhere, shadowing an otherwise sunny day. Sometimes clouds are like oversized cotton balls floating above us. At other times they are like sheets of paper in gray scale dimming the light of the sun. Before long, we wonder, *When will the rain come?*

Life is like that. Cloud cover is a routine part of daily life. Our day can start with fair conditions, but soon clouds appear and cast their dark shadows on our day. What appeared to be "fair" soon becomes "threatening," causing us to seek shelter from the coming storm. Let me ask you: are you struggling with rain today?

Notice the other picture Solomon uses. A tree has fallen in the field. Just as clouds are like the shifting and changing conditions of life's circumstances, trees fall like obstacles across the pathways of progress. Do you find yourself facing obstacles that interrupt, limit, and discourage your best efforts to live a satisfied life? If so, do you use these changing conditions as excuses for a poor quality of life? Don't let clouds of difficult circumstances overshadow the clear and important commitments of your life.

Aren't you glad Orville and Wilbur Wright didn't wait to fly until they had designed the perfect airplane? They were willing, against the odds and in the face of doubt, to risk failure to open the door to a new age of travel through the skies. What we enjoy as commonplace today is far advanced from the skeletal structures the Wright brothers called *airplanes*. Yet Orville and Wilbur's willingness to fulfill a commitment to fly was not overshadowed by difficult or adverse circumstances.

Don't let clouds of difficult circumstances overshadow the clear and important commitments of your life.

Can you imagine what must have gone through the Wright brothers' minds and hearts as they made their first ascent? Racing down the runway, risking the potential of disaster, raring back on the rudder, and then soaring from the familiar horizon toward the wonder of the heavens? What a moment of discovery—*flying!* The Wright brothers defied the law of gravity and experienced life in a new dimension. Their leap of faith paved the way for future generations to "look up" and discover life with new possibilities.

As Solomon nears the end of his search for satisfaction, he moves us toward a completely different conclusion than the one he initially presented. Solomon "pilots" our thoughts from the pit of bankruptcy to life in a new dimension. Solomon's challenge? When you hit bottom and have nowhere else to turn, look up!

3. Satisfaction Is Found in Accepting Our Ignorance and Acknowledging God's Rule

The third discovery Solomon made in his search is this: we gain greater satisfaction when we accept the fact that we live with many questions and only God has all the answers. "As you do not know what is the way of the wind, or how the bones grow in the womb of her who is with child, so you do not know the works of God who makes everything" (Eccles. 11:5).

Are you overwhelmed with questions? *Why did this happen to me? What should I do next? Where is God?* Remember, God is absolute and perfect in answers. Do you know God's mind? No. Can you fully know God's way? No. But anything we struggle to understand or endure has resolve in the providence of our all-wise and all-knowing heavenly Father.

Satisfaction is not found in what we get, what we do, what we know, what we have, whom we are with, or any of the other things Solomon has explored or searched along the way. Here is Solomon's ultimate discovery: God holds the answers of life. God is the solution. Satisfaction is not found apart from God!

Look at this verse again: "You don't know the works of God who makes everything." The message of the book of Ecclesiastes is eclipsed by the phrase *under the sun*. However, under-the-sun living does not satisfy, no matter how hard we try.

Here is Solomon's ultimate discovery: God holds the answers of life.

Solomon hits bottom as he declares bankruptcy in his search. He now knows the search for satisfaction he has so long endured is never to be resolved under the sun. It is God—the creator and sustainer of all things—who must be engaged if we want to find true satisfaction.

In today's language, Solomon is saying that we have a limited search engine if we confine our search to things found under the sun. Solomon looked up beyond the sun to Someone. Like Solomon, we must acknowledge our own inadequacy and our own personal bankruptcy in order to make life's greatest discovery. The secret to satisfaction in life is found in relationship with the One who made the sun, the One who shaped you in your mother's womb, and the One who has all the answers and applications for life. Satisfaction can never be experienced apart from Him.

Life must be lived in a dimension beyond the sun. Solomon wasn't referencing some mystical or ethereal spirituality; his reference is specific. It is "God who makes everything." If you know and trust this Creator God, your search is on track. If you do not know Him, your search will never end.

There is much you may not know about the winds or wonders of life. But make no mistake. It is God, the One who dwells beyond the sun, and who created the sun, moon, stars, and even babies in their mothers' wombs, whose name alone is the "password" needed to move a personal search from bankruptcy to discovery.

If we look back over Solomon's shoulder, we will discover he operated the vast majority of his search in a closed system of understanding and experience. Every search turned up inadequate at best and empty at worst. But here Solomon "Yahooed!" with his discovery that God holds the answers to all the questions and uncertainties that swallow life with doubt, frustration, and fear.

Each one of us must discover that there is deity beyond our limited humanity, and this God has revealed Himself in His creation, in our consciences, and ultimately in His Son, our Savior, Jesus Christ. Once you make this discovery, you can move from existence and experience to a life with purpose and satisfaction. This life is not only satisfying but fulfilling and thrilling. However, the prerequisite is bankruptcy. We must come to the end of our own self-satisfying search so that we can discover the satisfaction found in knowing God and enjoying Him forever.

Solomon looked up from the pit of his personal bankruptcy. And in that moment of potential despondency, he experienced new discovery.

We must come to the end of our own self-satisfying search so that we can discover the satisfaction found in knowing God and enjoying Him forever.

What about you? Are you running your search engine today, hoping to find some new solution? Have you added advanced searches only to find you are still living in search mode? You are not alone. People search and search but do so with no thought or concern for God. And the results have remained the same since the beginning of time. Apart from knowing God and discovering His purpose for your life, life will only be an unsatisfying search.

Satisfaction comes when we accept that we don't have all the answers and acknowledge God's rule.

4. Satisfaction Is Found in Embracing the Adventure of Life

The fourth life discovery Solomon made in his bankrupt experience is this: satisfaction is found as much in embracing the adventure of life as it is in accomplishing the goal.

Life is both journey and destiny. In an effort to find a destination of satisfaction, you can miss the joyous journey of discovery God has planned for you. Note these words of wisdom: "Be sure to stay busy and plant a variety of crops, for you never know which will grow—perhaps they all will. Light is sweet; it's wonderful to see the sun! When people live to be very old, let them rejoice in every day of life. But let them also remember that the dark days will be many. Everything still to come is meaningless" (Eccles. 11:6–8 NLT).

Life is not a game. The stakes are real, and loss can be catastrophic. At the same time, life is an adventure. Seeing the hand of

God and understanding His plan make every day a new adventure. Once we know and understand that our life is made by Someone beyond the sun, we can enjoy and embrace life under the sun. We can live life to the fullest, knowing that our Creator God is working His will and plan in our lives.

Instead of living with a checklist of "things to do before I die," develop a new list of dreams and desires to live your life in the glorious adventure of knowing and trusting your Creator God. When you do this, your life will be marked by joy in the journey and in the destiny.

This is quite a contrast to the compulsive drive of our age to do more and more—only to discover in the end that we have "been there, done that." We often wonder what else we can do to experience a satisfying life. Are you living under a to-do list that results in compulsive living without contentment? True contentment is found in knowing and doing the will of God.

True contentment is found in knowing and doing the will of God.

5. Satisfaction Is Found in Living to the Fullest Today

The final thing we observe from Solomon's list of life discoveries is this: satisfaction is found in living to the fullest today, not in rehearsing our yesterdays or projecting better tomorrows. He says, "Rejoice, O young man, in your youth, and let your heart cheer you in the days of your youth; walk in the ways of your heart, and in the sight of your eyes; but know that for all these God will bring you into judgment. Therefore remove sorrow from your heart, and put away evil from your flesh, for childhood and youth are vanity" (Eccles. 11:9–10). Solomon wants us to know that the way to live a life of satisfaction is to *live today*! Solomon's reference to a young man means, "The sooner, the better!"

The Message translates this verse: "You who are young, make the most of your youth. Relish your youthful vigor. Follow the impulses of your heart. If something looks good to you, pursue it. But know also that not just anything goes; you have to answer to God for every last bit of it" (Eccles. 11:9). Enjoy every day to the glory of God. This is what makes life worth living.

As I sit at my desk this morning, I am reminded of some wonderful yesterdays by the smiling faces and moments captured in the photographs surrounding my office. Parents, mentors, family, and friends all look at me as I engage this day of service and work. Some photos have now faded through time, and others are incomplete because of death. Each tells a story of some treasured event, occasion, or memory. Yet I cannot cling to my yesterdays no matter how good or how sweet they are to remember. Yesterdays are gone.

Then what about tomorrow? I can take my calendar and planner to project the things I hope to do tomorrow, but the calendar is changing, my clock is ticking, and life is ebbing away. These thoughts are but distractions for the opportunities and privileges of today.

I believe satisfaction in life is related to gathering a string of satisfying todays. As I focus on this day, I discover the joy of satisfied living in harmony with my Creator God and in fulfilling the nearest task at hand.

Are you in the pit of bankruptcy and despairing at the view from the bottom? Do the broad brushstrokes of disappointment, change, dissatisfaction, and emptiness color the portrait of your life today? Maybe they have come at a great price. They did for Solomon as well, but you don't have to stay at the bottom. Instead, when you hit bottom, look up!

a view from the bottom

Five Lessons from a Royal Bankruptcy

1. Satisfaction Is Found in Letting Go, Rather Than Holding On

"Give a serving to seven, and also to eight, for you do not know what evil will be on the earth" (Eccles. 11:2).

- Be generous in a world of greed.
- Show kindness in a world of callousness.
- Exercise faith in a world of fatalism.

2. Satisfaction Is Found in Our Commitments, Not Our Circumstances

"When the clouds are heavy, the rains come down. When a tree falls, whether south or north, there it lies. If you wait for perfect conditions, you will never get anything done" (Eccles. 11:3–4 NLT).

Don't let clouds of difficult circumstances overshadow the clear and important commitments of your life. When you hit bottom and have nowhere else to turn, look up!

3. Satisfaction Is Found in Accepting Our Ignorance and Acknowledging God's Rule

"God's ways are as hard to discern as the pathways of the wind, and as mysterious as a tiny baby being formed in a mother's womb" (Eccles. 11:5 NLT).

Here is Solomon's ultimate discovery: God holds the answers of life. God is the solution.

4. Satisfaction Is Found in Embracing the Adventure of Life

"Be sure to stay busy and plant a variety of crops, for you never know which will grow—perhaps they all will" (Eccles. 11:6 NLT).

Seeing the hand of God and understanding His plan make every day a new adventure.

5. Satisfaction Is Found in Living to the Fullest Today

"When people live to be very old, let them rejoice in every day of life" (Eccles. 11:8 NLT).

Enjoy every day to the glory of God. This is what makes life worth living.

You have made us for Yourself, and
our hearts are restless until they find rest in You.

—AUGUSTINE, *Confessions*

chapter 14

the secret to a satisfied life

Ecclesiastes 12

Words, like people, change with time. Today I am older than I was yesterday. I do not feel any different than I did five years ago, but the mirror keeps score. Each time I pass the scoreboard of life, I am reminded of the fact that change is under way.

I have noticed that words—our everyday vocabulary—also change over time. Words like *wallpaper, pods, hits,* and *mouse* have different uses than they did in my childhood. And then there is *spam.* When I was in elementary school, Spam was a hot commodity at the dinner table, but now spam is an unwanted commodity at the computer.

I am not sure how the word for that familiar spiced ham moved into the world of technology, but the term has redesigned its use in everyday vocabulary. Some suggest *spam* made its way into the Internet world through association with a Monty Python song, "Spam, spam, spam . . ." repeated ad infinitum. Like the song that will never end, electronic junk mail, or *spam*, demands your attention with unrelenting annoyance.

The term may also be traced to a group of students in a Southern California computer lab. These young techies associated Spam with the attitudes of a new generation toward that familiar lunch meat. No one eats it much anymore, they observed.[1]

Whatever the influence, the word *spam* is now the victim of our ever-changing world. The new "spam" lacks all the qualities and properties associated with the miracle of its first appearing. It describes a wanton and wasted use of energy, money, and technology for those who frequent the Internet. Today, spam is unsatisfying and useless.

Solomon contested some "spam" of his own in the ancient world. In fact, it was the time, attention, and effort diverted by "spam" that caused Solomon to express cynicism and despair toward life at the beginning of Ecclesiastes. Solomon's SPAM concoction is simple: Sex, Power, Achievement, and Money. Like the meat product of yesterday and the junk e-mails of today, the four components of Solomon's SPAM prove to be disappointing and unsatisfying pursuits in the search for satisfaction. Eventually, they all lead to emptiness.

For this reason, Solomon declared a radical conclusion from the beginning: "Vanity of vanities, all is vanity" (Eccles. 1:2). Have you come to the same conclusion? Are you dissatisfied with the SPAM of life?

Remember Your Creator

At the end of Ecclesiastes, Solomon gives guidance for a new beginning. Far from the cynicism and fatalism that shaped his first journal entry, he now has something to say about the source of satisfaction. He challenges us to shift our attention from SPAM to a new focal point. Let's observe: "Remember now your *Creator* in the days of your youth, before the difficult days come, and the years draw near when you say, 'I have no pleasure in them'" (Eccles. 12:1, emphasis added).

Solomon says there is a way to satisfaction in life. It is the way of God. Only when we acknowledge our Creator and our desperate need of a relationship with Him can we find satisfaction.

Ptolemy was an astronomer who lived in the fifth century AD. He sought to advance the world of his day through postulation and discovery. Ptolemy asserted that the earth was the center of the universe. For almost one thousand years, his point of reference was considered a scientific fact.

Only when we acknowledge our Creator and our desperate need of a relationship with Him can we find satisfaction.

However, in the fourteenth century, Nicolai Copernicus investigated Ptolemy's claim and found fault with Ptolemy's skewed calculations and limited development. His conclusion was this: the sun, not the earth, is the center of the universe. This discovery revolutionized the world of science and space. Until Copernicus, people lived with a false presupposition. However, once the correct center was discovered, the right conclusion was made.

After exhaustive investigation, Solomon found the correct center: life revolves around the Creator, not the creature.

What Is Your Focal Point?

What is your focal point today? Is it you? Is it your circumstances? Is it your relationships? Is it your bank account? Is it a possession? Or is it God?

If you want to find satisfaction in life, you must start by analyzing your focal point. If your focus is on anyone or anything other than God, then your search for true satisfaction will be frustrating and disappointing.

Golfers will never hit a golf ball on a path they are not focused on. If their focus (aim) is off, then it affects everything about the outcome of the game.

If your focus is on anyone or anything other than God, then your search for true satisfaction will be frustrating and disappointing.

What or whom are you focused on today? Are you seeking to find satisfaction apart from a relationship with God? Is He above and beyond all other affection, allegiance, and ambition in your life? If not, begin your search for true satisfaction by asking yourself, "Do I believe in God?" There are three fundamental reasons to believe in God. Let's look at each of them.

Believe in God Because of Creation

First, look at the beauty and variety of nature. What do you see? God's master plan and design. The universe is a highly complex and precise creation. From the movement of our fingers as they stroke the keyboard to the adjustment and peripheral vision of our eyes from one place to another, our bodies testify to the specific design of a Creator.

I cannot buy into the mind-set that human development is a result of catastrophic explosion and accidental progression. To say that plant life, sea life, human life, the oceans, mountains, and trees are all "accidents" of nature is the most unreasonable of all human propositions. It would be the equivalent of saying that a computer is the product of an explosion and progression of time in a parts factory. Yet today many schools have indoctrinated students with an all-encompassing presupposition of naturalism, teaching that life and the world in which we live are products of chance, motion, and time—with no consideration given to the wonder of a Creator.

Believe in God Because of Conscience

The second reason for you to believe in God is that you have a *conscience*. Creation surrounds you, but your conscience is something deep within you that longs for purpose and meaning in life. We all have a desire for significance as well as justice. While cultures, people, and sin have impacted the condition of the human conscience, we have a natural inclination within our conscience to distinguish between good and evil.

I am not a philosopher; I am a preacher. However, what I have experienced about human nature is that, for all of their failures and shortcomings, people crave a code of conduct and consequences for right and wrong behavior and for true and false values.

In his classic book *Mere Christianity,* Cambridge scholar C. S. Lewis describes how the evidence of conscience led him to faith in Jesus Christ:

My argument against God was that the universe seemed so cruel and unjust. But how had I gotten this idea of just and unjust? A man does not call a line crooked unless he has some idea of a straight line. What was I comparing this universe with when I called it unjust? If the whole show was bad and senseless from A to Z, so to speak, why did I, who was supposed to be part of the show, find myself in violent reaction against it? A man feels wet when he falls into water because a man is not a water animal. A fish would not feel wet. Of course, I could have given up my idea of justice by saying it was nothing but a private idea of my own. But if I did that then my argument against God collapsed too, for the argument depended on saying that the world was really unjust. That is, God is unjust. Not simply that it did not happen to please my private fantasies. . . . Thus, the very act of trying to prove that God did not exist (in other words, the whole reality of this world) was senseless. I found I was forced to assume that one part of reality—namely my idea of justice (or injustice)—was full of sense. Consequently, atheism turns out to be too simple.[2]

While the pain, suffering, and ugliness you see in the world may cause you to question or deny the existence of a good and loving God, your own sense of right and wrong, good and evil, justice and injustice denies such an easy out. Your conscience cries out for a quality of life associated with a higher standard.

Believe in God Because of Christ

The third and final evidence for believing in God that we will discuss is this: God revealed Himself through His Son, *Jesus Christ.* More than two thousand years ago, God stepped out of heaven and became one of us in Jesus Christ. The apostle John, who walked and talked with Jesus, wrote, "We have seen and testify that the Father has sent the Son as Savior of the world. Whoever confesses that Jesus is the Son of God, God abides in him, and he in God" (1 John 4:14–15).

So great is the influence of Jesus's life and teaching that the world has never been the same. He hungered and thirsted; He laughed and cried; He suffered and died. But His death was not merely a physical passing; it was a judicial sacrifice. First Peter 3:18 tells us that Christ died for us—the just for the unjust: "Christ also suffered once for sins, the just for the unjust, that He might bring us to God, being put to death in the flesh but made alive by the Spirit."

However, this is not the end of the story. Jesus Christ rose from the dead! He passed through the dark veil of death to a resurrected life, and He has forever satisfied the sin debt you owe to God. Christ died to taste death for you that you might experience life—full, satisfying life—through His name. You can know the Creator God in a real, vital, and personal way through His Son, your Savior, Jesus Christ. And to know Jesus is to know life in a new dimension. Jesus said, "I have come that they may have life, and that they may have it more abundantly" (John 10:10).

So what is your focal point? Focal point mattered to Solomon. He had to change both perspective and priority to begin his life on the right course toward a satisfying destination.

What Is Your Truth Source?

After declaring the need to *remember your Creator* at the beginning rather than the end of life, Solomon reminds us that we need to remember the importance of focusing on truth for life. "Because the Preacher was wise, he still taught the people knowledge; yes, he pondered and sought out and set in order many proverbs. The Preacher sought to find acceptable words; and what was written was upright—words of truth" (Eccles. 12:9–10).

Solomon wrote a journal to present truth in life and for life. We can learn by experience and observation and from other people. But most important, we can learn from God. The same Creator who made us gave us His owner's manual—the Bible. This manual provides us with the essential and fundamental truths we need for life.

I know this concept of truth—absolute truth—is tough in an age of negotiated agreements. The fundamental life principle of our day is this: If it is right for you, it is true for you. In this view, you become the source of your own truth. Truth can be spoken of only as a suggested progression of thoughts and experiences. The problem is that every day we are faced with the opposite of such reasoning.

This is certainly true in the physical universe. The law of gravity is not an idea or a suggestion. It is *law*. We can deny it as an unseen mystery, but we won't defy it. It is evident, exact, and consequential.

This is also true in the realm of mathematics at its core of design, development, evaluation, and measure. Math is an exacting science: one plus one equals two. Truth by its very nature is narrow.

And it is true in the social world. As we mentioned earlier, death is an absolute. That is why Solomon had to deal with it, and so do you.

Solomon spent a lifetime trading time for experience. In the end, he points to truth. For this reason, I, too, have staked my life, my hope, and my future on the truth of God's Word, the Bible. Just as I believe in the God of creation, I believe in His revelation and self-disclosure in the pages of Scripture. It is my truth source for life. The Bible has never been revised, but it is always right, relevant, and sufficient for our every need.

What Is Your Life Quest?

Not long ago, I asked an employee at Barnes and Noble how many books they carry in the store. He suggested somewhere in the vicinity of 250,000 volumes. Talk about needing a cup of Starbucks to cruise the shelves! Yet the reality is, if you read and read and read only to read words and gather information, you will still be empty. Knowledge is never sufficient. Reason is always limited. Learning is often inadequate.

Education, while important, has become the idol of idealism today for a full and meaningful life. But Solomon said it well: "Of making books there is no end, and much study is wearisome to the flesh" (Eccles. 12:12).

You don't need more knowledge, information, or skill development, even though all these have their place. What you need is *truth*. "The words of the wise are like goads, and the words of scholars are like well-driven nails, given by one Shepherd" (Eccles. 12:11). In the New King James Version of the Bible, "Shepherd" is capitalized in this verse to indicate deity. Why does this matter? Because apart from the knowledge of God found in the truth of Scripture, life is empty.

Education with the knowledge of God will lead to wisdom, influence, and life impact. But without God, education only leads to more questions, as it did for Solomon.

What is your life quest? What will you give your energies to? What kind of relationships will you build? How will you manage your schedule and priorities? What will be your standard to assess whether your life measures up?

Will you come to the same conclusion as Solomon? "Fear God and keep His commandments, for this is man's all. For God will bring every work into judgment, including every secret thing, whether good or evil" (Eccles. 12:13–14).

You can spend your life, waste your life, or invest your life.
You make the call.

That's it! You can spend your life, waste your life, or invest your life. You make the call. Solomon's choice was clear. His life quest would be to honor the Creator and to live a life of reverence and respect toward Him.

It is interesting that Solomon, in the book of Proverbs, picks up where he ended in Ecclesiastes. "The fear of the LORD is the *beginning* of knowledge" (Prov. 1:7, emphasis added).

What Is a Satisfied Life?

So what are the secrets of a satisfied life? Let me make it very simple:

- *Give your attention to the God who made you for Himself.* He has a plan and a purpose for your life. If you leave Him out, you have nothing left. Everything under the sun is "vanity" without Him.

- *Read the instructions.* So many of us are such "do-it-yourselfers" at heart that we never grow beyond our own limitations and opinions. Let God's Word reshape your mind, heart, values, and relationships. I suggest a daily reading of the Proverbs for a good dose of divine wisdom.
- *Live beyond yourself.* Many live only for themselves. The greatest way to benefit others is to follow the footsteps of men and women of faith whose lives and testimonies bless us today as they challenge us to believe.

There it is. Results. Real and lasting results for satisfied living. In the end, Ecclesiastes is a book that

functions not as a meal but as a bath. It is not nourishment; it is cleansing. It is repentance. It is purging. We read Ecclesiastes to get scrubbed clean from illusion and sentiment, from ideas that are idolatrous and feelings that cloy. It is an exposé and rejection of every arrogant and ignorant expectation that we can live our lives by ourselves on our own terms. The author's cool skepticism, a refreshing negation to the lush and seductive suggestions swirling around us, promising everything and delivering nothing, clears the air. And once the air is cleared, we are ready for reality— for God.[3]

chapter 14

the secret to a satisfied life

Solomon's SPAM:
Sex
Power
Achievement
Money

The four components of Solomon's SPAM prove to be disappointing and unsatisfying pursuits in the search for satisfaction. Eventually, they all lead to emptiness.

Remember Your Creator

"Remember now your Creator in the days of your youth, before the difficult days come, and the years draw near when you say, 'I have no pleasure in them'" (Eccles. 12:1).

After exhaustive investigation, Solomon found the correct center: life revolves around the Creator, not the creature.

What Is Your Focal Point?

Three specific reasons for personal belief in God:
1. Believe in God because of creation.
2. Believe in God because of conscience.
3. Believe in God because of Christ.

What Is Your Truth Source?

"The words of the wise men are like goads, and the words of scholars are like well-driven nails, given by one Shepherd. And further, my son, be admonished by these. Of making many books there is no end, and much study is wearisome to the flesh" (Eccles. 12:12).

We can stake our lives, hope, and futures on the truth of God's Word. The Bible is always right, relevant, and sufficient for our every need.

What Is Your Life Quest?

"Here is my final conclusion: Fear God and obey his commands, for this is the duty of every person. God will judge us for everything we do, including every secret thing, whether good or bad" (Eccles. 12:13–14 NLT).

You can spend your life, waste your life, or invest your life. Solomon's choice was clear. His life quest would be to honor the Creator and to live a life of reverence and respect toward Him.

What Is a Satisfied Life?

Give your attention to the God who made you for Himself.
Read the instructions.
Live beyond yourself.

When Christ reveals Himself there is satisfaction in the slenderest portion, and without Christ there is emptiness in the greatest fullness.

—ALEXANDER GROSSE, *on enjoying Christ*, 1632

chapter 15

satisfaction guaranteed

Ecclesiastes 12

There is nothing like a visit to New York City at Christmastime. Streets are lined with trees glistening with thousands of lights. Shoppers pause at storefront displays, clutching bags from Macy's, Saks Fifth Avenue, and Bergdorf Goodman's. The melody of "White Christmas" can be heard in the distance as street vendors sell hot dogs and pretzels. And wool-clad skaters glide past spectators at the base of a forty-foot-tall Christmas tree, the holiday icon of Rockefeller Center. New York City is indeed a magical wonderland of lights, sounds, smells, and movement at Christmastime.

I visited New York with only sixteen shopping days left until Christmas. But I wasn't there to shop. My time in the city was sobered by the dilemma of two lifelong friends, Harold and Judy, who were in a battle with cancer. Harold and Judy are people whose positive encouragement and generous investment of love in my life have made all the difference during the past twenty years. Their fight with cancer began in the summer, when Judy received a difficult diagnosis and traveled to New York in search of the best possible medical care and treatment for an unusual form of cancer. Then, with a turn of the calendar page, Harold discovered he, too, had a progressive malignancy that sent them back to the city before year's end.

It was one of those difficult seasons in life. Trouble came knocking, and two people I love answered the call with wisdom, hope, and faith.

I flew to New York with two other friends, Dr. Jack Graham and O. S. Hawkins. Whatever feelings of joy we had about being in New York at Christmas were tainted by the fact that Harold and Judy, people who had spoken into each of our lives through their love, were facing one of life's darkest hours.

The trip was brief but memorable. The surgery, I am grateful to say, was successful. But another event was shoved into the schedule of these days that marked my life as well.

Two days before our scheduled departure to New York, Michael Jenkins, executive director of the Dallas Summer Musicals, attended our annual Dallas Christmas Festival at Prestonwood Church. In a brief encounter with Michael, he mentioned he was involved in a new Broadway production entitled *Brooklyn: The Musical*. And then he added, "Call me if you have any plans to visit New York."

We told Michael of our planned visit to be in the city and of our brief stay. He urged us to take time to see the musical; with the evening open before the day of surgery, we did.

Brooklyn: The Musical is the story of a young woman's search to satisfy her longing to meet the father she never knew. Her mother had a love affair with an American soldier on tour in France, but his departure and subsequent silence left her with a child whose only clue to her father's whereabouts is in her name, Brooklyn. The mother, worn and scarred by pain, takes her own life, and young Brooklyn begins a search to find her American father.

Her search takes young Brooklyn, a talented vocalist, to performance halls in New York and to the streets of Brooklyn. There among the street people she encounters many who share a search to find satisfaction in life. While every story and experience is different, the yearnings are still the same.

Brooklyn meets a street singer who reminds her there is a story behind every face and a hunger deep within every beggar's heart she meets in the street. He sings, "There's a heart behind these hands. There's a soul beneath these clothes. There's a story behind these empty eyes that no one wants to know."[1]

A heart. A soul. A story that speaks to every one of us.

Where Will We Find Satisfaction?

The issues we have discussed all relate to issues of the heart. The soul is the deepest part of us, the part where we can know and commune with God. And there is a story, a script written while our clock is ticking that is colored by all of the ways we have searched to find satisfaction.

This is the search that Solomon expressed, and it is the search people make every day—the drive, the desire, and the determination to find meaning, purpose, and satisfaction in life. Whether we live uptown like a king or down-and-out in the streets, we all thirst for true satisfaction.

Where will we ever find it?

This was the search of a woman who met Jesus on a street near a well. In Scripture she is identified only as being "a woman from Samaria." This woman had an empty heart, a hole in her soul, and a story that, as Jesus probed, was not one she wanted everyone to know.

A woman of Samaria came to draw water. Jesus said to her, "Give Me a drink." For His disciples had gone away into the city to buy food. Then the woman of Samaria said to Him, "How is it that You, being a Jew, ask a drink from me, a Samaritan woman?" For

Jews have no dealings with Samaritans. Jesus answered and said to her, "If you knew the gift of God, and who it is who says to you, 'Give Me a drink,' you would have asked Him, and He would have given you living water." The woman said to Him, "Sir, You have nothing to draw with, and the well is deep. Where then do You get that living water? Are You greater than our father Jacob, who gave us the well, and drank from it himself, as well as his sons and his livestock?" Jesus answered and said to her, "Whoever drinks of this water will thirst again, but whoever drinks of the water that I shall give him will never thirst. But the water that I shall give him will become in him a fountain of water springing up into everlasting life." The woman said to Him, "Sir, give me this water, that I may not thirst, nor come here to draw." (John 4:7–15)

The problem faced by the woman at the well on that hot day so long ago is the same faced by people you pass in the streets every day. From the streets of New York to the suburbs of Dallas, from the inner city to the most remote community, people thirst. We all have "holes in our souls." We search for satisfaction, but the satisfaction we so deeply crave is not found in the things we accomplish, the possessions we accumulate, or the experiences we accentuate.

Satisfaction is found in knowing and experiencing God through a relationship with His Son, Jesus Christ.

The Password Is *Jesus*

How can you find satisfaction? Is there any guarantee? Yes. Solomon pointed to the source. "Let us hear the conclusion of the whole matter: Fear God and keep His commandments, for this is man's all. For God will bring every work into judgment, including every secret thing, whether good or evil" (Eccles. 12:13–14).

Satisfaction is found in knowing and experiencing God through a relationship with His Son, Jesus Christ. The password to accessing satisfaction in life is *Jesus*.

When you put Jesus's name in the search bar of your life, you will quickly find that all the other misguided and inadequate searches are replaced by One who is the ultimate solution.

> The woman said to Him, "Sir, give me this water, that I may not thirst, nor come here to draw." Jesus said to her, "Go, call your husband, and come here." The woman answered and said, "I have no husband." Jesus said to her, "You have well said, 'I have no husband,' for you have had five husbands, and the one whom you now have is not your husband; in that you spoke truly." The woman said to Him, "Sir, I perceive that You are a prophet. Our fathers worshiped on this mountain, and you Jews say that in Jerusalem is the place where one ought to worship." Jesus said to her, "Woman, believe Me, the hour is coming when you will neither on this mountain, nor in Jerusalem, worship the Father. You worship what you do not know; we know what we worship, for salvation is of the Jews. But the hour is coming, and now is, when the true worshipers will worship the Father in spirit and truth; for the Father is seeking such to worship Him. God is Spirit, and those who worship Him must worship in spirit and truth." The woman said to Him, "I know that Messiah is coming" (who is called Christ). "When He comes, He will tell us all things." Jesus said to her, "I who speak to you am He." (John 4:15–26)

Think about this simple statement: *Jesus satisfies.* It is so simple it reminds us of a slogan on a T-shirt. It is like a message you might read on a church marquee as you pass by.

Yet to say Jesus satisfies in no way trivializes the seriousness of

His life, work, and ministry. He came to satisfy His Father's will. He came to provide the satisfaction of the righteous requirement of a holy God. There is nothing more essential to learn as the full meaning of these two words: *Jesus satisfies.*

For this reason, I can close this book by saying, "Satisfaction guaranteed!" Why? Let's look at two reasons.

Jesus Satisfies the Holiness and Righteousness of God

First, Jesus satisfies the holiness and righteousness of God. Before you start imagining a "feel-good" Jesus—a heavenly water boy sent to fetch you some fulfillment—you must be sure you understand the fundamental importance of who He is and what He came to do.

Jesus is the Christ, the Messiah, the one and only Son of the living God. He came to fulfill a divine mission, purpose, and plan. He came to die on the cross for your sins. By this act, He has *once for all* provided a full and satisfactory sacrifice for you (Heb. 10:10). It is your sin that separates you from the God who made you for Himself that you might know and experience Him. It is sin that parches the human soul.

What is sin? Sin is living ignorantly, independently, or defiantly apart from the knowledge and service of the God who made you for Himself. Evidence and expressions of sin are abundant in the world. The impact and injury of sin are thirst, emptiness, and a lack of satisfaction in the human soul. This is why it is so important that you recognize that sin is offensive to God. There is only one way to satisfy the righteous standards of a holy God: through the person and work of His Son, your Savior, Jesus Christ.

This was the ultimate discovery of a guilt-stained and sin-scarred Samaritan woman and her friends, who said, "We ourselves have heard Him and we know that this is indeed the Christ, the Savior of the world" (John 4:42).

Maybe you are thinking, *Why is this such a big deal? I know the story of the passion of Jesus Christ. I believe in Jesus.* Many do, but many of us lack understanding and personal acceptance of the seriousness and offensiveness of our sin before a holy God.

Here is where you must start—with God and not with yourself.

God will judge all human work. This is a fact you cannot ignore. Solomon made it clear numerous times in his journal. One day each of us will give an account of our actions before God, the righteous Judge (Rom. 14:12).

Let's review Solomon's final words again. "Let us hear the conclusion of the whole matter: Fear God and keep His commandments, for this is man's all. For God will bring every work into judgment, including every secret thing, whether good or evil" (Eccles. 12:13–14).

Here is where you must start—with God and not with yourself.

The issue of your human satisfaction is inseparably linked to knowing, experiencing, and living in vital relationship with the Creator God, who made you for Himself. And this relationship begins when you agree with God on the subject of your own sinfulness, accepting the fact that you can never satisfy the holy standards of God by your own effort. Only when you experience His forgiveness—made possible by the payment of Christ for your sins on the cross—can you be made right with God.

Why the cross? Two reasons. First, *sin incurs debt with a righteous God.* Therefore, "without shedding of blood there is no remission [payment for sins]" (Heb. 9:22). Second, *the debt of sin is death.* In other words, sin carries a death penalty. Thanks be to God that the gift of God is eternal life through Jesus Christ our Lord. Jesus paid it all. Jesus satisfied God's righteous requirement for you. There can be no satisfaction in your life apart from Christ.

Therefore, the first essential for satisfaction in life is that you

begin with Him. You must start with this conclusion: getting right
with God is the starting point for everything else that matters. You
must understand, acknowledge, and accept God's standards and not
try to establish your own.

You must begin where God begins with the issue of human sin.
You are responsible before God for your attitudes, actions, associations, and activities. Not a pretty picture, is it? But starting at the
conclusion—making peace with God through the Lord Jesus
Christ—you are ready to live life to the fullest. Jesus satisfies the
holiness and righteousness of God for you.

Author and Bible teacher Alistair Begg recently said, "All God
wants has been achieved and all we need has been accomplished *in
Christ*. He is righteous!"[2]

Jesus satisfies!

Jesus Satisfies the Hole in Your Soul

The other essential guarantee is this: Jesus satisfies the hole in
your soul.

Many years ago, I heard Adrian Rogers quote the lyrics to a
somewhat obscure gospel song:

> Friends all around me are searching to find
> What my heart yearns for by sin undermined.
> I have the secret, I know where it is found,
> Only true pleasures in Jesus abound.

Jesus not only satisfies the holiness of God; He alone satisfies
the hole in the human soul.

Two thousand years of history provide evidence of this reality
as Christ-followers place their faith and hope in Him. From the distant shores of the remotest mission fields of the world to high-
impact, highly developed cities, the testimony of every true believer
is captured in the words of Alexander Grosse found at the beginning

of this chapter: "When Christ reveals Himself there is satisfaction in the slenderest portion, and without Christ there is emptiness in the greatest fullness."[3]

This was the newfound melody in the heart of the empty and thirsty Samaritan woman. John goes on to tell us that she "left her waterpot, went her way into the city, and said to the men, 'Come, see a Man who told me all things that I ever did. Could this be the Christ?'" (John 4:28–29). In the end, this woman with a worn life, a dry bucket, but a brimming heart exclaimed, "I have found true satisfaction!"

Jesus Christ satisfies the holiness of God, and He fills the hole in your soul.

And this is my prayer for you. Don't waste your life with ritual and routine searches under the sun. If you do, you will only confirm the words of wise King Solomon, "Vanity of vanities! All is vanity." No matches found. It was the conclusion Solomon provided from the start.

However, Jesus Christ satisfies the holiness of God, and He fills the hole in your soul. Instead of wasting your life, you can spend your days living life to the fullest and serving the purpose of your Creator God, who made you for Himself and has a significant plan and purpose for your life.

Satisfaction guaranteed!

> *But as for me, my contentment is not in wealth*
> *but in seeing you and knowing all is well between us.*
> *And when I awake in heaven, I will be fully satisfied,*
> *for I will see you face to face.*
> −PSALM 17:15 TLB

satisfaction guaranteed

"Let us hear the conclusion of the whole matter: Fear God and keep His commandments, for this is man's all. For God will bring every work into judgment, including every secret thing, whether good or evil" (Eccles. 12:13–14).

Where Will We Find Satisfaction?

We search for satisfaction, but the satisfaction we so deeply crave is not found in the things we accomplish, the possessions we accumulate, or the experiences we accentuate.

"Thou hast made us for Thyself, and our hearts are restless until they find their rest in You."
—Augustine

The Password Is Jesus

Satisfaction is found in knowing and experiencing God through a relationship with His Son, Jesus Christ.

"I have come that they may have life, and that they may have it more abundantly" (John 10:10).

"These things I have spoken to you, that My joy may remain in you, and that your joy may be full" (John 15:11).

"These are written that you may believe Jesus is the Christ, the Son

of God, and that believing you may have life in His name" (John 20:31).

Jesus Satisfies the Holiness and Righteousness of God

Through His death, Jesus satisfied God's righteous requirement for you. There can be no satisfaction in your life apart from Christ.

- Why the cross?
- Sin incurs debt with a righteous God.
- The debt of sin is death.

Jesus Satisfies the Hole in Your Soul

"The woman then left her waterpot, went her way into the city, and said to the men, 'Come, see a Man who told me all things that I ever did. Could this be the Christ?'" (John 4:28–29).

Like this woman with a worn life, a dry bucket, but a brimming heart, when you meet Jesus, you can exclaim, "I have found true satisfaction!"

"But as for me, my contentment is not in wealth but in seeing You and knowing all is well between us. And when I awake in heaven, I will be fully satisfied, for I will see You face-to-face" (Ps. 17:15 TLB).

Your Search
A Personal or Group Study Guide

Chapter 1: Living in Search Mode

1. What observations have you made about life from your own personal search for satisfaction?
2. If you could break any pattern of monotony in your life, what would it be?
3. What is your greatest dissatisfaction in life?
4. What disappointments have you faced in your efforts to live and lead a more satisfying life?
5. Who do you know who is living life on the high end of the satisfaction scale?

Chapter 2: No Matches Found

1. How did you score on the Life Satisfaction Scale presented in this chapter?
2. How do you think Solomon would have scored?
3. Can you list some "myths of satisfaction" you have experienced in your life?
4. Why do you think so many popular life searches leave us empty?
5. Have you limited your search as Solomon did to life "under the sun"?

Chapter 3: Life Happens!

1. Have you ever considered your use of time as you would your use of money?

2. If you reviewed your "expense account," what would be your primary debt or investment?

3. How are you doing with personal time management?

4. What words would you use to define the season of life you are in today?

5. Where do you need to apply the phrase "Life happens, but life is not just happenstance"?

Chapter 4: My Clock Is Ticking

1. What do you want the "dash" between the bookends of life ("a time to be born and a time to die") to read?

2. How would you define your life purpose?

3. What areas of your life call for greater wisdom in the management of your time?

4. Of the "Five Ways to Maximize Your Days," which one has the greatest application to your life today?

Chapter 5: "Do-it-Yourself" Attitudes

1. Can you think of a specific "do-it-yourself" moment that turned to disaster?

2. What did you learn from this experience?

3. In what areas of your life have you avoided asking for assistance?

4. Who are the friends you can count on in life?

Chapter 6: Pride and Precipice

1. Can you identify shadows of pride in your personal relationships with others?

2. How has your pride affected (or infected) you?

3. Who needs your help to advance in life?

4. What steps can you take to move beyond yourself and help make a positive difference in the life of another?

Chaper 7: The Friendship Factor

1. Do you consider yourself a loner or someone who enjoys friendships?
2. If you are a loner, what hinders you from having friendships?
3. Do you have friends who "stick closer than a brother"? Who are they?
4. Which of your friends increase your productivity? reduce your vulnerability? provide safety? increase your security?
5. What kind of friend are you?

Chapter 8: Random Reflections

1. Are you a religious person?
2. Would you describe your religion as doing good deeds to gain God's favor?
3. Do you have a relationship with God or just a religion?
4. Are you seeking to satisfy your needs through religion, money, someone, or something?
5. Do you often ask, "Why am I not satisfied with everything I have?"

Chapter 9: The "D" Word

1. Do you think of your death as something that will occur far in the future when you're old and sick?
2. Would you do things differently if you knew you would die next week?
3. Do you view death as an end to existence?
4. Do you view heaven as a place where only good people go?
5. Are you certain you will go to heaven when you die?

Chapter 10: Simple Pleasures

1. How would you list the "simple pleasures" in your life?
2. Look at your list. Have you experienced your "simple pleasures" today, this week, this month, this year? If not, why?

3. Does your list reflect elements of relaxation, contentment, or accomplishment?

4. Imagine yourself rediscovering your list in your sixties. As you read it from the perspective of a senior adult, is there anything you would change?

Chapter 11: When Life Seems Unfair

1. Do you tend to compare yourself with others—their joys, talents, opportunities, experiences, difficulties, and so on?

2. Can you easily rejoice with people over their successes, or do you inwardly begrudge their achievement as if it is unfair to you?

3. Do you view hardship as defeat, or are you able to see past the difficulty to future successes?

4. Do you allow your past to keep you from reaching your potential?

5. How do you address the challenges you face with your own unique abilities?

Chapter 12: Wisdom's Sampler

1. Do you pray for wisdom before making decisions?

2. How do you discern between what is good and best when the answer is not immediately evident?

3. Since foolish behavior is linked to what is contained in the heart, do you allow your heart to be exposed to foolish inclinations, such as the denial of consequence, the presence of deceit, or the belief that you can hide, ignore, or outwit God?

4. Do you read the Bible on a regular basis to fill your heart with God's wisdom and instruction?

Chapter 13: A View from the Bottom

1. Do you frequently find yourself searching for something—something that satisfies, something better—to fill a vacancy in your life?

2. Where are you searching?
3. Is your knowledge about God through experience or from what you've heard others say about Him?
4. Each morning, do you acknowledge the day as a gift from God to live in harmony with Him?

Chapter 14: The Secret to a Satisfied Life

1. Would you say your focus centers more on God, yourself, or others on any given day?
2. Do you seek to find satisfaction apart from a relationship with God?
3. Do you believe in God?
4. If you are seeking satisfaction in life, are you willing to look beyond this world and believe the One who holds the answers to true satisfaction?

Chapter 15: Satisfaction Guaranteed

1. Do you want to experience the satisfaction that only God can provide?
2. Are you separated from God because of your sins?
3. Do you want the penalty of your sins erased through Jesus Christ's payment on the cross? Do you want to be forgiven of your sin and have a right relationship with God?

notes

Chapter 2: No Matches Found

1. Claudia Wallis, "The New Science of Happiness: What Makes the Human Heart Sing?" *Time* 164, no. 3 (January 17, 2005), A3. Reprinted with permission.

2. Ibid., A5.

3. Ibid.

4. Ellen Goodstein, "Unlucky in Riches," *Bankrate.com*, November 8, 2004, http://www.bankrate.com/brm/news/advice/20041108a1.asp (accessed June 15, 2005).

5. Bill and Melinda Gates Foundation, "Foundation Fact Sheet," http://www.gates-foundation.org/MediaCenter/FactSheet/default.htm (accessed November 28, 2005).

Chapter 3: Life Happens!

1. TURN! TURN! TURN! (To Everything There Is A Season). Words from the Book of Ecclesiastes. Adaptation and Music by Pete Seeger. TRO—© Copyright 1962 (Renewed) Melody Trails, In., New York, NY . Used by permission.

Chapter 4: My Clock Is Ticking

1. Michael J. McCarthy, "Time Running Out for Clockmakers in Chicago," *Wall Street Journal*, February 6, 2005.

2. *Webster's New World College Dictionary*, 4th ed. (Cleveland: Wiley, 2004), s.v. "fatalism."

3. Adrian Rogers, "Sermon on Psalm 118:24," sermon delivered to Bellevue Baptist Church, Memphis, TN.

4. Andrew Nash, "J. M. Barrie," in Robert Clark, Emory Elliott, and Janet Todd, eds., *The Literary Encyclopedia* (London: Literary Dictionary Company, 2001), http://www.litencyc.com/php/speople.php?rec=true&UID=5138 (accessed June 15, 2005).

Chapter 5: "Do-It-Yourself" Attitudes

1. Wikipedia: The Free Encyclopedia, s.v. "Howard Hughes," http://en.wikipedia.org/wiki/Howard_Hughes (accessed June 15, 2005).
2. John Maxwell, *The 17 Indisputable Laws of Teamwork: Embrace Them and Empower Your Team* (Nashville: Thomas Nelson, 2001), 2.

Chapter 6: Pride and Precipice

1. Zig Ziglar, *Zig Ziglar's Secrets of Closing the Sale* (New York: Berkley, 1985), 22.

Chapter 7: The Friendship Factor

1. Gary Smalley, "DNA of Relationships," http://www.dnaofrelationships.com/therevolution/getinvolved.html (accessed December 3, 2005), excerpt from chapter 1 of *The DNA of Relationships* (Wheaton, IL: Tyndale House, 2004).

Chapter 8: Random Reflections

1. "Car Hood Pops Open, but Men Keep Driving," FloridaToday.com (April 1, 2005).
2. Robert Service, *Collected Poems of Robert Service* (New York: Penguin, 1940), 3

Chapter 9: The "D" Word

1. Taken from *When You Can't Come Back* by David F. Dravecky, Janice Dravecky and Ken Gire, Jr. Copyright ©1992 by Dave & Jan Dravecky. Used by permission of the Zondervan Corporation.

Chapter 10: Simple Pleasures

1. Jack Graham, *Marriage by the Book* (Plano, TX: Powerpoint Ministries, 2004), 15.

Chapter 11: When Life Seems Unfair

1. Lindsay Terry, ed., *Stories Behind 50 Southern Gospel Favorites* (Grand Rapids, MI: Kregel Publications, 2005), 1:197.

Chapter 12: Wisdom's Sampler

1. David Templeton, "Box of Love," *North Bay Bohemian*, February 5–11, 2004, http://www.metroactive.com/papers/sonoma/02.05.04/dining-0406.html (accessed June 15, 2005).
2. Warren Wiersbe, *Be Satisfied* (Wheaton, IL: Victor Books, 1990), 119-120.

Chapter 13: A View from the Bottom

1. Walt Kaiser, *Ecclesiastes: Total Life* (Chicago: Moody, 1979), 113.
2. Ibid., 114.

Chapter 14: The Secret to a Satisfied Life

1. "The Spam Story," http://www.cusd.claremont.edu/~mrosenbl/spamstory.html (accessed June 15, 2005).

2. C. S. Lewis, *Mere Christianity* (New York: HarperCollins, 2001), 38–39.

3. Eugene Peterson, *The Message* (Colorado Springs: CO: NavPress, 1996), 354–55.

Chapter 15: Satisfaction Guaranteed

1. Mark Schoenfeld, "Heart Behind These Hands," *Brooklyn: The Musical*, Razor & Tie, 2004.

2. Alistair Begg, unpublished data.

3. Alexander Grosse, *on enjoying Christ* (1632) quoted in Charles Haddon Spurgeon, *The Treasury of David: Spurgeon's Classic Work on the Psalms* (Grand Rapids, MI: Kregel Publications, 2004), 325.